THE NEXT TEST OF MEN

A Spoken Word Joint

By

Rudwaan

Copyright © 2015
All rights reserved

No portion of this work may be reproduced or used in any form for profit or gain without the author's prior expressed and explicit consent

Author: **Rudwaan**
Publisher: **Move The Village**
Website: **http://www.thelionstale.com**

Edit and format by

Rudwaan

Manuscript prep by

Kiambi Thompson, Apple Thompson, Karlene Thompson, Egypt Moiye

Cover Design by

HRU
http://www.GetSeenAndHeard.com
678-871-SEEN

ISBN: 978-0-9900279-1-1

CONTENTS

Livications and thanks
Pre-word
Who This Is 10
 Their God Fears Us 11
The Same Thing 14
Poisoned Fruits 16
Ah! Sweet Tobago 20
The Making of Jack 21
Who Really Got You? 22
The Next Test of Men 25
We Buy Our Own Bullshit 26
Ready or Not 29
Chew On This 33
Let Them Cry 34
We Scare The Children 36
Brothers In Pain..37
Dear Miserable Whiteman 39
Amen 40
Pray 41
We Prey Now 43
 Under is Power Over 46
 You Thug Black 50
 You Reap and Grow 53
 Let The Children Play 54
Homie 57
The Book of Annaijh 59
Boys in The Hood 63
Enemy In Me 65
Brother 2 Brother 68
Bury The Dead 71
Dogs of War 74
Wait Wind!! 77
All for Shit 79

CONTENTS (cont.)

Eat Shit and Die 81
Know Thyself 82
Fences and Rusty Nails 83
Question It 85
Each Brother Matters 86
After-Thoughts 87
This Damned Nation 88
Cross-Over Poet 92
The Low on Their High 96
Shake Those Bones 98
The Season To Reason 101
Fear No More 104
Grow The Children 105
Saga of The Black Stone 107
No Thanks 110
Shades of View 111
Dues To Love 113
Pledge of Allegiance 114
Passion in The Night 115
Let Us Be 117
Body Parts to Body Bags 118
When Doves Cry 120
A Parting of Ways 121
Days of our Lives 122
There's More 123
Math of 2 Pillars 128
I Grow Weary Sometimes 129
We Be Angels 131
The Greatest of These 133
The Way of The Soul 136
I Speak of Ma'at 137
Questions of our Time 138
The Winds of Change 143

CONTENTS (cont.)

Against The Law 145
Here I Am 148
Show Me 150
Thru The Valleys 152
Sour or Sweet 155
The Blood 156
These Times Test Us 157
Pure Yang 160
Warrior or Soldier? 161
We Were One 163
Tangled Web 166
We Badly Pray 168
Are we Romans Yet? 170
Tweet This 173
Ye Be Gods 176
Sooner or Later 177
Me, Myself and I 178
This is for The Birds 179
People on The Bus 180
The Poet's Way 183
Martin Beyond 186
Truth Rises 191
Black Mother Spirit 194
Turn Right at The Light 197
I'm Just Saying 198
Rise Up 200
The Dinnertime Man 203
Queen 205
The Art of Noise 206
So Far 207
New Pages Are Born 208
Our Support Supports 209
Hypocrites 210

CONTENTS (cont.)

Surprised Again 211
The Cast-Aways 213
The Sea Saw Me 214
The Struggle Continues 215
Awareness 217
Natural man Awake 218
Brother's Keeper...219
Sow Your Seeds Well..221

LIVICATIONS & GRATITUDES

Livicated to the memory of those Africans slain by the 'run-away slave catchers' known as American Police

Livicated to the living Black souls who continue to struggle daily for the true liberation and re-ascension of the African culture.

Livicated to the Black womb-man who is the power-source of the Black man in this realm

Livicated to the Black man who knows this truth and pledges his life in protection of the Black womb

Livicated to the Black youth who reach for truth and refuse to accept a facsimile

Gratitudes to Karlene, Kiambi, Apple and Egypt for preparing this manuscript out of a handwriting that only a mother could love

Gratitudes to graphics designer Jimi Figz of GoldenRoseCreative.com for his contribution along the way to my final choice of cover designs

Gratitudes to professional photographer and magazine lay-out artist and designer Ras Moiye for his constructive criticism and ongoing encouragement

Gratitudes to graphic designer He Ruler for his professionalism and excellent customer service in designing this cover

Gratitudes to the Most High designer of my mind and body and the mother womb Irene that brought me thru

ABOUT THE TITLE

The title of this book is reflected from the Spoken Word piece that bears its name and appears on page 25. The inspiration for this work was drawn from the knowledge of who we as Black men truly are, and what our most supreme duty must be in this earthly realm, and that is to protect the Black womb of men. Should Black men truly tune into this responsibility we will see a drastic reduction of crimes against the Black woman committed by the Black man. When the Black man is reminded and remembers that his power-source in this realm is the Black woman then how he relates to her will improve fundamentally.

We know that the maafa and the ongoing oppression's wounds have done much to ravage the natural relationship between the Black man and the Black woman, we must also accept that the fissure between the two began long before the Popes issued Papal Bulls to Europe to enslave the African into perpetuity. For the African to re-ascend to their rightful place as gardeners and caretakers of this planet and depose the current bastards who have the planet on the brink of nuclear disaster, global warming, and untold poverty and suffaration all so that a few greedy European families can pretend to be gods, the Black man must wake up and reconnect and recommit himself to the Black woman.

This is essentially 'THE NEXT TEXT OF MEN' While the words written within are not necessarily solely for enjoyment, but rather for elucidation and repudiation, upliftment and correction, they are written with an enjoyable flow and design.

THE NEXT TEST OF MEN

Who this is

I am an ebony pen
writing in ebony ink
thinking in ebony thoughts
thoughts to make you think
                              I am inside your ebony mind
                              minding you like my business
                              reminding you who this is
                                  this is my thesis
                                    a catharsis
                                unlike the cathexis
                          of those who are catechist
                  those who claim to be like Christ
         who promote and profit from crisis to crisis
                      they don't know who Christ is
            they cry crocodile tears for the crucifix
I am a linguistic catalyst
I come to start some shit
vernacularly assault the bullshit
I bring devastation to the cultural corruption
a solution to the pollution of your mental station
                so read these words carefully
                      please pay attention
      you've had the Old and the New Testament
           now comes the Next Test of Men
                          I am
                     an ebony pen

<u>Their Fair God Fears Us</u>

They fear their god
for their god is a fair god
a god who thrives on their fear
a god fair in skin
like the whiteness of the void
a god to avoid
short in temper
easily annoyed
drawn from the darkness
tried and failed to possess it
so now opposes it
oppresses it
suppresses it
kidnapped and enslaved it
claims to hate it but is envious of it
their god is a jealous god
rebellious and vengeful in nature

Their god who is a fair god claims to hate sin
to him all that is dark is sin
like the darkness of the African skin
so says their fair god whom they fear
this is the god they taught us to fear

They say their fair god died for our dark sins
but they lied about our dark skins
so they sent missionaries
to spy on our dark continent
to offer salvation
to a people born in sin
born in dark skin
heavy in melanin
the same stuff
the universe is made of
so to him
the universe is made of sin

This vengeful, jealous, fair god
offers to wash our dark sins
to dip our dark skins in his blood
and make our dark sins
as white as snow
or straight to hell we go

So now we fear his fair god
and hate our dark skin
his fair god covets
the wealth of our melanin
in our dark skins
his fair god covets
the wealth of resources
found on our dark continent

while we come now discontent
forevermore to repent
for sins committed against us
by their fair god who fears us

    This fair god wants to be dark
    so why do you fear this fair god?
    why do you fear his wrath?
    rifts in the matrix
    has us launching life-rafts
    their truth reads like comedy
    you have my permission to laugh
    for their fair god fears us.

The Same Thing

Our ancestors said to one
there's nothing new under the sun
cells lay dormant waiting to become
                    to be initiated into the cycle of osmosis
                           the give and take of life
                             some say Isis and Osiris
                                those who truly know
                    will tell you who Auset and Ausar is

Those who have gone before you will guide you
they know what you feel and why you feel it
they say love it but be ready to leave it
to go within is to go where the journey begins

        For your journey is one that ancestors have thread
                                    some were froed
                                     some were bald
                                   some were dread
                they listened when the Most High said
                        you're in the god phase now

You are never alone young warrior
we all been through the same thing
the same thing been the same thing
since the dawn of the same thing
some died of the same thing
some tried to do the same thing
some even failed at the same thing
yet others excelled at the same thing
we were all confronted by the same thing
and in that moment we all knew the same thing
we were made of the same thing

Born of the same fabric
we knew then
that we will never be alone
this is the way to the god phase
we were becoming one with The One

That same thing is the way
the way to manhood
for manhood is the way
to your God-hood
manhood is taking responsibility
for the primary role of a man
to protect the womb-of-men
        this same thing has been the same thing
                since creation
        you are not alone young warrior
            you are not alone.

<u>Poisoned Fruits</u>

                              Our children are our ancestors
come now to question our answers
some say the children have lost their minds
others say they have no soul
that their music reflects
a disconnection from the whole
we must ask a different question
to arrive at another conclusion
for our children have come
to question our answers

The children are indeed fruits of the tree
poisoned fruits though some may be
so too must be the tree
look to the roots for the truth
for there we find the soil, the culture

                      We as an Afrikan people were uprooted
transported then transplanted like livestock
removed from a soil that favored our growth
nurtured our potential to be
a soil rich in spirituality, social responsibility
replanted on plantations as chattel stock
made to labor like beast of burdens
and to eat like them
what fruits would come from this?

The Afrikan soil was slowly being poisoned
made acidic, for the beast lives only to eat, shit,
multiply then die, the destruction of Afrikan civilization
was as intentional yet instinctive as a dog lifting its leg
and pissing against a tree, it is in the nature of yurugu
to piss against the tree of life
what fruits would come from this?

A soil richly alkalinized with harmony was slowly
being acidified, wars of outright destruction for
destruction's sake were waged, wars to dominate,
colonize and enslave the Afrikan soil was being made
to their liking, they were like pigs in a pigsty

Harmony was modulated into noise, music is but a
manifestation of our functional unity, this noise was
driven into our Afrikan soil causing disharmony at the
root level, what fruits would come from this?

A people functionally unified may encounter violence
but they will be difficult to enslave effectively
effective enslavement requires isolating and
terrorizing the individual, making the individual
to feel that they are all alone, that they need not fight
such a people will eventually become like sheep
guarded by one sheep-dog, feeling powerless to fight
since each sheep sees itself as one on one against
that big bad sheep-dog, it does not occur to a flock of
sheep that they out-number the sheep-dog, such is
their nature, can those sheep then give birth to sheep
that fight for their freedom?

When the tree is compromised what then is expected of the fruits? Our children have come to question our answers. We are out of harmony with each other because we are out of harmony within ourselves. We have no love for self so we have no love for each other. What fruits would come from this?

This foreign acidic soil has eaten away at our roots, our systems for drawing life giving sustenance from a total environment that understands the Most High, that stands under the tutorship of Tehuti, regulated by the divine laws of Maat. Once we were divided and spun out of harmony within and without, each saw themselves as the way, each tribe viewed itself as the nation, wars broke out inter-tribal, unaware that they were fighting against themselves, each tribe chanted "my way or the highway", disharmony, disunity was now in the soil, what fruits would come from this?

It was child's play for Yurugu to introduce acidified ideologies disguised as truths. Religion was the tool used to introduce further lies to be accepted as truths. We were beaten black and blue, brought low to grovel like broken dogs then religion was applied to our oppression's wounds like salves to open flesh.

We were told to look for our redemption in the by and by, our savior would come from the sky, our soil was becoming more acidic, what then must come of the fruits?, would they not be born sour and forced-ripe? Would the music they make not reflect this acidified reality? Truth of our heritage in time replaced by the lies of histories.

Because we knew not the truth, the whole truth and no-things but the truth we could not effectively seek her protector her companion, justice, so our children have no peace. They come then like poisoned fruits.

Ah!! Tobago Sweet

Earth welcomes the morning sun
cocks crow, sleep done
blood flows, Island in motion
whole Island rises as one
a new day begun
children off to school, maids come
calypso music blasting from roadside props
roti shops prep, farmers tend to crops
noonday heat meets hungry bellies eat
a seaside bath is the main treat
everybody wet with sweat
but all you see is bright smiles and teet'
'good-day' is the daily greet
to everybody we meet
to the not so fortunate we sharing mango meat
this is Tobago life oh! how sweet
the day slowly crawls to a slow stop
daily danglers with thumbs up looking for drop
families called to sup brush teet' wash up
children to homework, TV news for grown-ups
bedside prayers for all
as night creatures echoes final call
before head hit pillow and body meet sheet
start sleep
ah!! Tobago life how sweet

The Making of Jack

Many have compromised their values
sold out to the evil doers amongst us
they look like us so you excuse them
make excuses for them
say they gotta eat
never mind that
they're eating us
robbing and carjacking us
so you say be strong just jack them back
so now we have a community of Jacks
jumping Jacks
like crabs in a barrel cracking backs
Black backs
the original jack nowhere to be seen
visits crime scenes
stars on big screens in "the making of Jack"
don't ask them for jack
they'll tell you look Jack I ain't got jack
pull yourself up by your own bootstraps Jack.

<u>Who Really Got You?</u>

Brother 2 brother young G I ain't trying to mock you
what I gotta say to you today may shock you
this Black on Black banging
got us all on the clock too
that sister's only nine
but she's doing time on the block too
no safe place to play
mama's mind on the crack too
fathers doing time for that time
he didn't take the time
to watch his back too

Now here you come strapped
187 on your mind too
but that other G got a gluck too
the system's after both of you
with eyes in the sky
all they do is watch you
somebody who look like you lied to you
told you how to do the what to do
now sirens blaring
pants sagging
gun tossing
but still they got you
now who got you when they get you?
who you thought got you
ain't there to get you
you get it?

This ain't the time young G
for me to tell you
get on your knees and pray
nor am I gonna tell you
simply hang tough thru come what may
cause right now we just talking
ain't nothing really popping

        Mama told me a long time ago
        friends can take you
        but they can't bring you
        young brother answer your droid
        I'm trying to ring you
        bring you
        some science to help you avoid
        that thing
        they got waiting for you

        It's not too late to see
        who's always been hating on you
        but it's not really you they hate
        it's because at your core
        you are really great
        and if you see that know that
        you'll forever change
        how you relate
        to the system
        in your state of not-knowing
        you're food to them
        I know you think you got one up
        but you come like fools to them

They don't care how hard you come
you ain't old school new school
you are no school to them
        a brother that would kill his own
           is a tool to them
                to use you and abuse you
                when you look for justice
                    they refuse you
                  this behavior of theirs
                  should not confuse you
              I know you're young brother
                but old enough to see
              we ain't trying to lose you

        Now pull your pants up
        and so pull your mind up
check the box that says "life I choose you"
            and brother
I know you haven't heard this in a long time
          but we love you.

The Next Test of Men

There be paid men
trained to act like made men
they profile and arrest men
more often than not they be us men
so be careful men

And confess then
who be the best men
they who test men
or they who best the best test of men
press against all odds then impress men
suppress men
who oppress men
then suggest then

That after the Old and the New
comes The Next Test of Men

That not all men be boys made to mend
some be born again seven times men
torn from the matrix by sages sent to warn men
that the best men
must protect the womb-of-men

We Buy Our Own Bullshit

I remember
when 1990 was the future
boys fought over girls
now they shoot you
they assault you
with all manner of deadly words
then they pull piece on you
blast you in the back
then throw peace sign at you

These are the days in the negative
the ways and means in the times that we live
give us now our daily bread
as we seek to move ahead
but fail instead
to real-all-eyes
that our salvation lies
behind us
beyond the days
of the Spanish invaders
and Columbus
who come bust us
into many many colonies
generating generations of inter-familial crisis
forgive us now our deadly sins
for we know not where this tale ends
and ahead begins

Forgive us
our sons and daughters
forgive us
and ahead begins

Who raises his voice in the East? ((In the East? In the East?...))
that is not echoed in the West
and how is the West the best coast
when the East is the host
to the rising suns?
our sons and daughters

Walk the street like wannabe gangstars
talk the talk of ill-nana pranksters
these are peeps
lost in the beats
of these
wannabes
mentalities
I say
this whole gangstar shit
is more hypes than realities

For sure
there's some stickup thugs out there
doing some really bad things
but the sad thing is
they're doing it to themselves

then they don't even feel right
for deep into the midnight
they wet their beds and they cry
dear momma, dear momma
is there a heaven for a gangstar?

Then like highly commercialized niggas
we respond to the dramas
but brothahs and sistahs
brothahs and sistahs
we're not gangstars
just consumers
performers
on this auction block of a stage
where we sell our rage
too the highest bidders
           then like dogs returning to its own vomit
                  we buy our own bullshit
                      we take it home
                we feed it to the children

              Who regurgitate the same bullshit
                        all over again
                              I say
                    I remember when
                    1990 was the future
                    boys fought over girls
                          and now…

<u>Ready or Not</u>

I remember when
in the days of children
we would play then
and say then
you go hide
and I'll come seek you

And as children do
we did
I would count to ten
while you hid
and we would play our games
all day long
ignoring time
till the setting sun
begging him to stay with us
to play with us
just one more hour
as grandmas yell
echoed through the woods
time for supper

And we knew what time it was
without a time-piece
we knew the hour was at hand
for we were the children of the play
the children of the times
and we knew the signs
the sun

Slowly closing his eyes
taking with him the daylight
water frogs croaking incessantly
welcoming the night
crickets chirping
Bats taking flights
grandmas yell permeating
like a microphone
calling all the young players home

And it must have been a naturally known fact
for all of nature seemed to join in the act
as creatures great and small
echoed their own final call
and we knew what time it was
Time now for the last play of the day
this play set our nerves on edge
for on this play we had no time
to do it again
we had no time
to screw up

For now
the sun was like a red ball of fire
falling from the sky
and grandmas final call
would find I and I
And so
you went to hiding
as I started counting
we knew what time it was
for it was on
the final countdown had begun

And like Tehuti's horn
sounding thru the heavens
my yell of ten trumpeted thru the trees
and like all of a sudden
all
was perfectly still

As if in anticipation of some rapture
this was the final chapter
this is the moment we played our whole day for
as more and more
the sun slowly died in the west
only to rise in the east
where Kilimanjaro rests

And I heard
the sound of the evening wind
rustling through the trees
as I lifted my voice
and screamed against the impending night

READY OR NOT!!
HERE I COME!!

and I found you
now the game was over
and so was the day
For the tone of grandmas yell
found us and told us
she won't be yelling no more
and we knew what time it was
it was time to go home

But this prosaic feature
is not about children's games
not about natures night creatures
nor grandmothers yelling names

This trek down memory lane
is a wakeup call under cover
an alarm sounding
calling us from under the covers
a warning of soughts
that it's time to get up

For the signs of the times
are here, there, and everywhere
and just like the games that children play
the night will soon end
and the sun will rise again
sending its brilliant ray of hope
his brilliant strategy for a new day
to seek us
to find us
to lift us up
will be found ready?
or
not?

CHEW ON THIS

Many a men dem treat woman like she bubblegum
flavor done
trouble come
dem pack and run
dragged from sidewalk to sidewalk
she now feel she stuck on he shoe bottom
stepped on and stepped over then finally scraped
life smacks her in the face with her mistakes
the skin she in she now come to hate
but it's not too late

Stella got her groove back so can she
how, she ask, she end up on the bottom of a shoe?
when he first met her she was queen
now she just another boo
well here's my advice to she
never let a man chew she out
this way her flavor last forever

Let Them Cry

Rush not to hush
that child that cries
who cries not for Biggie big macs
snoop doggie dogs
nor murder king fries
who cries but for love

Love spoon fed to his hungry soul
through spoken words and deeds
designed to make him whole
for unlike fast foods and empty lyrics
love will stand the test of times
will elevate his mind
above and beyond
this mine-field of a system
genetically engineered
to ensure his destruction
so rush not to hush that child

Let his cries be heard
on every corporate mountain top
where those who have successfully sold-out
hold-out
and without a doubt forget
that they are still in the valley of dry bones
let him cry

Let his cries be heard
thru-out those holly-hoods
where those man-made stars
fall further and further away
from heavenly thoughts
let him cry

Let his cries be heard
up and down those boulevards
where brothahs sell sistahs poison
graduate from prison
then go platinum
let him cry
let him wail
let us join him
and cry ourselves
awake

We Scare Our Children

We entrust the minds of our future
to the offsprings of the oppessors
yet expect them not to think inferior
and be furious

And as they think inferior
why would they not feel inferior
and be furious

And if we turn to the offsprings of the oppressors
and ask them for their civil rights
their equal rights
are we not reinforcing that feeling of inferiority?
and will these children not act inferior
and be furious?

Will the children not believe
they are inferior
and be in fear?
are we being fair?
we rehash lies told as bedtime stories
spun from his stories not ours
when we scare the children to sleep
do we not lay awake in fear of these children
who awake in fury?
how many watts must burn?

Brothers In Pain

I'm all for brothers looking out for sisters
and sisters looking out for sisters
but pray tell me
who's looking out for brothers
besides the police
please somebody tell me
who's watching our backs?

When back to back attacks unfold
tales of suffering Black souls goes untold
who feels my black silent pain?

When James Byrd Jr. is beaten
by three white men in Jasper Texas
strapped to a truck and dragged
as the paved road chain-saws his limbs
then he's be-headed
and Sunday morning finds us jumping and shouting
who feels our Black silent pain?

When Abner Louima is wrongly caged
staged like a wild animal
in a zoo-like lock down
violated from behind
by New York's finest clowns
who feels our pain?

When brother swings in the wind
like a broken limb
hanging from an age old tree
who feels me?

Who eases my pain
my Black silent pain
who will take my back
take me back?
beyond the days of Black on Black attacks
like the Black stabbing the Black in the back
and no one cares
no one shares

Why must a good Black man
be like unto a dead Black man
when will we stop stabbing each other
in the back
and start easing each other's pain
in the back?

We can't afford another day
in this damned valley
fighting over scraps
like stray dogs in back alleys

Now I'm all for brothers looking out for sisters
and sisters looking out for sisters
but who feels a brother's pain
our Black silent back pains
Shouldn't we?

Dear Miserable Whiteman

Hollywood says
you can leap tall buildings in a single bound
move faster than the speed of sound
even faster than Usain Bolt
grab live wires not even a jolt
journey thru worm-holes and back
you play the Mexican, the Indian you even play Black
you were in the beginning even before the beginning
you were Cleopatra, Moses even Gods and Kings
you not only received the ten commandments
you were in the burning bush that gave it
you are the Gods of wind and thunder
you can even breathe under water
you are the Jesus in the Christ
the men not the mice
roll the dice
you're the six twice
all others are but crap
only you can be Bond, James Bond
Idris is just a Black fish in a White pond
you are the conqueror of worlds and universes
you are the issuer of blessings and curses
this all plays well on the big screen
but in real life you are still the recessive gene
dear miserable whiteman you're facing extinction
life is not Hollywood this is truth not fiction
you're at negative population growth
so in the end your bullshit floats
dear miserable whiteman
now leap that.

Amen

We're running out of time
time for men who play men
say they are men
too many damn stray men
when did we stop saying amen
started sharing our women
with strange men
it's high time we stop getting high
and start seeing eye to eye again
somebody say
Amen

Pray

In the soul of the warrior stirs the mourning
as this day is born then torn
between love and labor
love for the play of the day
labor for the sight in the night

See now the newborn
who clings to Jacob's ladder
descending the very rungs of hell
to tell the devil 'let my people go'
then ascending each in turn to teach
the truth of our ancestral earth-rite
the soul of the warrior stirs

And like Yohanne the baptizer
crying in the wilderness
whispering spoken words like dew drops
on every sleeping flower
and showers our mother
our nature
with renewed vigor
let us pray

Pray
that the message be heard
before the night discovers its loneliness
and seeks to recover the sun

Pray
that the poet's rhyme
be to the elders like a fountain
and to the youths
like a truth serum

Let us climb now
to the top of the mountain
as we the chosen choose
like those who chose
like Ra-Moses

Come now this red sea of knowledge
here Jah's commandments
submerge our thirsty souls
in Abraham's bosom
that we may emerge
humble and wholesome
as the warrior mourns

Not for his personal loss
but for those who paid the cost
in the deep stillness of the night
as days and nights unite
into six million ways to die
one death
a debt paid for in full
with the blood of the warrior
here now his last breath
and awake

We Prey Now

We pray now
that our sins be washed
as white as snow
or straight to hell we go
but if our sins be white
are they still not sins?
the brainwash is deep within
as we pray now

We struggle tooth and nail to integrate
we consider ourselves fortunate
we can now go to their schools
and learn to trick poor families
out of their real-estate
as we graduate
from one degree of unrighteousness
to another
then we celebrate
as we prey now

We strive to be politically correct
as we neglect our own
for the company of pretentious asses
running for the same political offices
our ancestors ran from

we think we can change their system
but their system changes us
as we reach into our polished bag of lies
and rationalize
this capitalistic system of usury
where promissory notes are lied for
and died for
as we prey now

Forgive us our debts
as we forgive our debtors
like those scheming back-stabbers
those poisonous drug dealers
federally sponsored Black leaders
those psychic network tele-evangelistic healers
who justify the means
by the end$ they make
send them all this message

That we will not forgive them their debts
that we will testify against them come judgement
let them pray now

We will not remember how many homeless they fed
but how many they made homeless
how many they mis-led
let them pray now

We will not remember how many toys
they distributed in the hood
but how many Black boys
they stripped of good
as their playgrounds became war zones
send them all this message

That we will testify against them
in the end
as they pray now
for the end.

<u>Under is Power Over</u>

Journey then like Sojourner
to the under
for there is the power
and the glory
the beginning of our story
forever and ever
amen.

Many a men be mentors
mending broken souls gone astray
sending spoken words around the way
that even the fallen angels must obey

Be then like the high seas
when peace be still
raging waters fall to their knees
standing under the Most High
they aspire to become sky high
then return as showers of blessings
issuing forth from mighty clouds of joy
hear then this torrential down-pour
the happy wailing of that baby girl
that baby boy
and understand me
the blind will not see

That without understanding
wisdom will not be born
souls be forever torn
            gone with the wind
            like that designer label
            building without sight
            like that tower of babel
            they babble on
            while Cain slays Able
                      dispensing utterance
                      with much eloquence
                      but their words be fable
                      witness then
                      the plight of the dumb
                      like that wretched overseer
                        soon to be overcome
            like the deaf they will not hear
            the warning clap of the thunder
            eruptions of meditation from under

Where third-eye sees the way to trance
dance with fire and not burn
earn degrees not of this world
            where flesh be in it
            spirit not of it
            love it
            but be ready to leave it
            the blind will not see

That all things that be
comes from under
like the quake that quickens
her thighs asunder
for under is the womb
that gives shelter
unto whom we must return
then, now and after

Under is the science that birthed the subs
the marines
those dreaded seal teams
they stand under radar
they see
but cannot be seen

Under is the way to the throne
the way that leads back home
the way we lost
when stripped of culture
ripped from her womb
by that wingless vulture
shipped in shackles
mothers moaned for the fetus
tricked into powerless religions
our science used to defeat us
but understand me
the blind will not see

That under is the world of no-things
that houses dreams of all things
for all things that be
be but dreams
visions manifested
illusions tried and tested
                    and like dreams
            all things must cease to be
        once the dreamer ceases to dream

                    We be the dreamers of this world
                        the children of the under
                          and she calls us by name
                            for we've been too long
                                just getting over
                                    too long
                                just surviving
              blowing from one fashionable hype
                                  to the next
                        like leaves in the wind
              dearly beloved
              truly it's not over
        til we journey like Sojourner
                to the under
            for there's the power over

You Thug Black

What you're trying to do
was tried before
everybody fishing for their own fish
most everybody poor
              those that caught a little rich
                got no keys to the door
                so they can't let us in
                  it's not their house
                they're only visiting
thinking the road to success
is to be just like them

              So you buy white as you thug black
            black blocks on lock as you mug black
                    you drug black
                so black minds can't Sankofa
                  they can't reflect back
            sistahs killing seeds feeding needs
                  for that damn crack
                but you ain't no fat cat
                    just a black rat
        you ain't no gangstar
        just another prankster
        your whole life's a joke
          you refuse to invest
            so you die broke

A gangstar takes care of his own
      he looks out for his home
           your baby mama can't get a favor from you
                  much less a loan
      all your children are State owned
you say you're a gangstar?

      A gangstar don't shit where he eats
      don't spit where he sleeps
      and what's more important
         you can't either

      A real gangstar makes sure
those who look like him eats well
      this way
           nobody wants to run and tell
           nobody curses his soul to hell
children play safely in his streets
      neighbors got issues
      he squashes beef
      his streets are clean
      no hoes strolling
      no drug dealing

Now everybody else's streets are fair game
he'll sell them everything from car parts to cocaine
      that was then
now he sells houses and airplanes

                              now here you come
                           like a broke down dog
                       licking your massa's plate
                               licking his balls
                                kissing his ass
                      making him even more great
bell-hopping his luggage of left-over heritage
discarding your own
you come now a junior mafia
no longer Shaka now Capone
                       you think you eye-talian
                                  you mook
                             you're just a clone
                                  a clown
                          a wannabee mini-me
           you're not even as worthy as his dog
                  you're just the goddamn bone
                 soon to be buried in his backyard

You Reap and grow

Search yourself frequently and you should find
that time waits not for mankind
the ideals that existed as they were,
are no longer what you are looking for
as you learn, you grow, as you grow, you must learn
how to maintain and build on that new growth.

Life often seems like a heavy burden, but this is due entirely to knowledge that has become accessible to you, and now it is up to you to log into that particular channel and absorb the knowledge awaiting you. Once you have absorbed life's lesson you grow up.

You have now afforded yourself the strength, mentally and spiritually speaking, twice or more times, that which you had. Logically since you are stronger, or more aware, everything seems lighter, or easier to deal with—until your next period of growth. Unless you are fully aware of your own strength or knowledge, it is possible that a mountain can be created out of a mole hill. Take the time to sit down and allow the force that is supreme within you to inspire a great deal of your thoughts, I'm sure that you will realize that anything that is possible can be achieved, but you must take the necessary steps to make it happen. In the end you reap what you grow and as you grow.

<u>Let the Children Play</u>

                        Like lost souls
              on this raging and angry sea
                  we come now to be
                      but not to be

                                            Playing with feelings
                                          like wind me up toys
                                          nurturing mentalities
                                    like little girls and boys

Mind trapped in the days of let's play house
we be playing games
even with sacred vows

                Oh we be frontin' like we be playahs
                while claiming not to be haters of them
             but someone sure as hell hates the children
                    for they be dying everyday
                                        and if we feel
                                      like we say we feel
                                          then we know
          that they be the true playahs for real
so let the children play
as we come now to be
                      but not to be

Students of ill-conceived universities
that lack the curricular abilities
to elevate us spiritually
instead
    they abort us like bad votes
     casting us into this world
   to play life for promissory notes
to these ends we vibrate
thru out our lives
this musical discord resonates
so we came now to be
    but not to be

  Shapers of our destinies
  workers of righteous deeds
  sowers of god-knowledge seeds

So the children seek to assume our roles
  like lost ships at sea
we bury them in the blackest of holes
     where they see nothing
      they feel nothing
      they hear nothing
    so they aspire to be nothing

But how can they find their way
when we the builders seek to play
how can the children lead
when they need to feed
how can they embark
on that journey to elevate the spirit
when all they know is street wit
I tell you this

We must come now to be like saviors
but not to be like playahs
on this raging and angry sea

Homie

Brothers need to stop treating sisters
like something they own
like them headphones in their ear
yeah, the ones pumping that bullshit in the air
making you feel large while your sister's in fear
you fear the power of the sister
so it's the sister you fear
back to them headphones
what you own you can do with as you will
you can throw them in the air and shoot to kill
when you grow a pair you can foot the bill
them headphones you can trash them, bash them
you own them so you can crash them
but our sisters? the womb of men?
our power-source at that?
like the portal that brought you from this to that?
now you think you phat?
you can't bash that
that's against the Law
don't get it twisted
I'm not talking about the law you saw
the ones with guns, badges and a thirst for war
I'm talking about Divine Law
I speak of Ma'at
the Law that was before the law that is
Yurugu's broken law that is

that broken tool
sharpened by token coons
the law you bow to so you are broken two
your father more than likely is broken one
                                              where it begun
                                          it's not that far back
                                    study The Laws of Ma'at
                              bash the sisters you bash that
                        and you don't want that to bash back
                    you say you god but you bashing Black
                    Black backs are tired of getting whacked
              whipped stripped tarred feathered and hung
  who are you to stop the sister from singing her song?
brothers need to stop treating sisters
like something they own
take off them damn headphones
turn around head home
I think you left your head home
homie.

The Book of Annaijh
Chapter 9: Strong Medicine

The Preacher said
God reached down
and took her
at the age of nine
God chose to close
life's book on her
God being God
could have simply withheld
life's breath from her
but instead to her
God sent to her
a bullet to the precious and tender head of her

But I disagree with this preacher's account of her
for God didn't issue a recall that day on her
didn't wake with her
and decided to expand the heavenly hosts with her
no holy ghosts and sons
longed for the company of her
no Mr. Preacher
I disagree with your account of her

I count her years on ten fingers
and I'm left with one remainder
          a reminder
       that we the village
     failed to raise the child in her
    now we raise our voices sing songs
      and praise the child in her
light candles, hold vigils
and recall the *oh so few days* of her
            caravans of cars and busses
              lead to graveyards
             where we bury her

But let's not bury our heads in the sand with her
less we fully account
for why this happened to her
we'll be caravanning again and again
to bury another and another
        Annaijh died because
      we the village
        failed
    to raise the child in her

We failed her with our silence
    while evil hustled and grinded around her
        we chose to honor codes
         that tells us not to tell
         that evil swells and dwells
      around her
      raising hell
      around her

We failed her with our ignorance
as we ignored the violent weeds
growing around her
threatening the life of this *yet to bloom* flower
we valued them weeds
more than we did her
them weeds pay the rent
with pillaged paper peddled
from exploiting children just like her

We failed her with our impotence
rims and dogs carry more importance than her
them rims get our undivided attention
see them spin and shine with brilliance
we'll never see the full brilliance of her
them dogs are well groomed
well fed
well cared for
single mothers struggling on welfare
who cares for?
fathers ignore
for the company of dogs
walking them
talking to them
playing with them
their children left
to play on their own

where are the fathers
to watch over them
watch out for them?
to praise them as they play
to encourage them
like they "that's a good boy" them dogs

We the village failed to raise her
above them rims and dogs
now Annaijh is dead
with a bullet to the head
by one of them dogs
no Mr Preacher
God didn't take her

We the village sent her
it takes a village to raise but one Annaijh
let's not fail the others
let us move the village

8/2007

Boys in the Hoods

                              A man-child was born
                              to a man-less woman
                                        screaming
                    grows and is told of days of old
                                     eyes gleaming
                         caught up in half-truths
                      with the neighborhood troops
                                      now teaming
                  running with fatherless boys in the hood
                                     up to no good
                                  always scheming
                        Just before manhood
                           legally entangled
                            now jail-bait
                          three years upstate
                          comes now probate
                              can't wait
                          back on the street
                             can't compete
                            a growing hate
                          heart turns to stone
                         young brother's alone
                              can't relate
Now he walks the streets day and night
groping
mama's in the pews on her knees
hoping
comes the blue-eyed beast in blue
cruising the hood
scoping
sees young brother on his knees lost in space
doping

Just another nigger to tag they said
let's make him pay
back in the system
forced to rat out
forgot how to pray
overcome with hate
killed his cell mate
nothing to say
led to the chair
still don't care
his final day

Little sister in front yard
with her best friend
jump-rope skipping
mama in the kitchen
sausage and pancakes flipping
comes the pay-back boys on drive by
glucks and uzis clipping
little sisters no more
best friend dead for sure
hood ripping

Thrown to the dogs
ways of the righteous
forsaken
our man-children are without guidance
will the fathers awaken?
or will the roots of our future be forever shaken?
comes the day of reckoning
take control of our future
or be taken

Enemy In Me

This poem has no entertainment value
it points three fingers at me one at you
with thumbs up to the Zulu crew
this poem seeks to unsettle the mind
to have us restless
best yet
to accuse us of being too damn complacent
in this land of ill-opportunity

This poem will not incite you to laughter
matter of fact
standing ovation will be denied
first inclination is to protect false pride
second is to say truth lied

This poem points the finger inside
it cites the enemy in me
it recites I and I are to blame
for our wretched condition
our despondent position
for we are but a foolish people

We who were once architects of pyramids
seers of stars
now erecters of crack houses
slaves to strip-bars
men once gods-to-bees
now street corner hustlers
gangstar wannabees
scavengers in the midst of this concrete jungle
pushers of chemical ills and woes
that turn our daughters to hoes
sporting gold chains claim like Hannibal
but I consider it criminal
to sell your sistahs crack
and other assorted mind attacks
creating tombs of the wombs
where you plant seeds to fertilize
unborns delivered then to a den of lies
like uncertain heirs to your bastard throne
    is it any wonder they seek only to destroy
then die?
the blame is on I and I

Now of some sis I say this
for some sis be no sis
but his miss
to use as his mistress
then dismiss
leaving her with nothing but her shame
I say I and I are to blame

For we be not like kings and queens
but deposed
relegated to the ranks of corporate America's hoes
judged worthwhile by their counterfeit degrees
like favorite pets distinguished by pedigrees
we strive to serve the enemy in me

But from this poem we will not hide
let the enemy in me be identified
for we war not with sticks and stones
not against flesh and bones
but against unseen forces
bearers of unholy crosses
where now are the prophets
the bearers of truth
the word warriors
the very elect
selected from the very beginning
for there-in was the word spoken
stand I say
and be like unto the chosen
for there is a war in heaven this day
and if heaven be in me
then so is the enemy

Brother 2 Brother

This poem has no entertainment value
it is not designed to make you laugh
jump and shout or clap your hands
no
this poem will piss you off
for in this poem
I take issue with you brothers

For who of us spoke the word
then brought themselves into objectivity
out from subjectivity?
who of us has blessed themselves
with their own creativity
willed themselves from captivity?
these be issues I have with you

For if the lion feels like a sheep
then sheds its mane
will his mane not grow again
will he not remain the same
in the eyes of the sheep?
or should creation rearrange
their perception of the truth
to suit the feelings of the lion?
these be issues I have with you brothers

And if a group of liver cells decide
to hell with life as a liver cell
we will function alternatively
consequentially
will this not lead to cancer of the liver
then ultimately
death to the whole body?
then who grants us the rite
to choose our own sexuality?
was the Spoken Word "in the beginning"
not good enough for us?
brothers I must tell you this
for I have issues with you

Somethings are Just beyond our damn control
like creation of the whole
for over four hundred years
we were forcefully twisted and bent
and now
you bend over sideways, front ways, all kinda ways,
and deliberately subjugate yourself
unto another man

So I ask you
how can positive energy
combine itself with positive energy
and expect electricity?
I say brothers I have issues with you

For these are not the days to be bending over
for back doors are just exits
like where the shit flows
not where your manhood goes
which of us dare ignore
the law of relativity
and not die consequentially?
like valuable Jets you fall from the sky
then dismiss it as a tragedy
but like fools you ignore the ramifications
the indwelling checks and balances
which unleashes divine consequences
when you give into your weak emotional indulgences
none can escape the Judgement of broken laws
as your wickedness breakout like open sores
look I say to instances of mal-physical manifestations
as evidences of your spiritual contamination
brothers
I have issues with you

Bury The Dead

                        Let us not follow them
                into the void of their inhumanity
                   avoid then their insanity
             their hunter and prey mentality
         they be the victims
     who mistake their own identity
        who like vultures
  feed on their own vulnerability
holding down corners
they come now trapped
like Pavlov's dogs
conditioned to react
        shoot first ask questions later
            hear them bark
            hear them rap
       let us not follow them.

        They who slither like snakes to and fro
             casting spells on their own
                   with chemical woes
      scattering seeds of mayhem
     shattering dreams for the system
    they be servants of the grim reaper
     who turn our mothers to weepers
        let us not follow them

They shit on our minds
with base lines and gangster rhymes
dropping albums like A-bombs
they destroy our future
with words of plutonium
as we consume their bullshit
then watch them go platinum
for their game is to be sold
while the truth goes untold
let us not follow them

Those dis-educated dis-cultural fools
say we be worthless
less we integrate yurugu's schools
they rally to the lies of Western studies
that does naught but supplant
ancestral memories
graduating cum-last-again
we hold fast again
to their counterfeit degrees
let us not follow them

As they give their souls
to this the land of the wrong and restless
and as the world turns
one by one they are sifted
culturally shifted
into no-man families

Separated like oil and water
they cry alone
no queen in his home
no king to call her own
so the children look to Barney for food
the remote control fine tunes their attitudes
mal-adjusting their moods
as lies are told to their vision
rites of passage abandoned
in exchange for Yurugu's concept of religion
let us not follow them
instead
let us bury the dead

Dogs Of War

Time is up
for moving our feet
to that pied pipers beat
for while we bump and grind
empty lyrics permeate our minds
black heads are bounced from bank to bank
crack dealers on the corner giving thanks
Blacks trap Blacks then rap
'god blessing all the trap niggers'
but a brother that would trap another
is a bitter nigger trying to be bigger
                         a negro who needs to grow
                         soon to reap what he sows
                                    time is up

We who were once architects
now subjects of government housing projects
like branded stocks
        they relo us like unfit welfare rejects
                Black-heads are bounced from
                                      trap houses
                                  to court houses
                                    to jail houses
                            to half-way houses
                        yet we ask what's up?

                              Time is up for games
                             games that people say
                                that people play
                               be they ball games
                                    war games
                                   mind games
                                it's all the same
for games are but a time-out from real-time
and it's high-time we realize
that in these times
                  we are at war
              we are at war for our balls
                  our manhood

    Yet we spend all day perfecting that jump-shot
    news breaks at six another brother shot another
                  another family on the streets
                    cause they ain't got a dollar
night falls and darkness finds us
playing bitch for the cops
then we rob us
history is a lie
so we lie when we shout
                give us Barabbas
             while casting our votes
             for those who harass us
             and yet we ask what's up?

Time is up for sleeping
for creeping
on our hands and knees
begging
for that government cheese
their counterfeit degrees
our spiritual clock strikes midnight
bats take flight
while deep in the valley of dry bones
comedians seek to stir with laughter
the poet's words finds the minds they're after

The musicians instruments serenades the angels
they feel our pain
then shed their tears like rain
I hear heavens bells
dogs of war screaming in hell
come now knowahs floods of knowledge
sweeping through the valley
as one by one we live
give us now our due bread
for we who slept like the dead
scream
time!!

Wait Wind!

My fellow revolutionaries
Sojourners of truth
others
lend me your ear
for I feel the winds of change
arising on the horizon
and I am aware

Aware that those yet asleep
in this valley of misguided devotions
will be eternally separated
from our blessed congregations
but fear not

For this is not a poem about fear
Nor is it a poem about doom and despair
but rather this poem beckons those still awake
to say it a little louder
to cut it a little deeper
to shake those dry bones a little harder
to not be concerned
about whether what we say will pay
for this is not the time
to be concerned about your time
but rather
these times ought to concern us
I say

(((Wait Wind!!)))

don't blow just yet

For these are the times
in which one of ten Black men
    the HIV is positive of its victims
        wait wind

These are the times
in which our little Black boys
are choosing the style of coffin
    they wish to be buried in
        wait wind

These are the times
in which Black families are becoming extinct
where the Black woman
    must be queen and king
        wait wind

These are the times
in which the blackest Panther must roar
and our voices must mount up
as on wings of eagles and soar
soar to the highest mountain top and shout
    shout into the night

(((Wait Wind!!)))

don't blow just yet
for yet another day we may hear you
and awake

All For Shit

Say brothuh
what is you selling?
your biznazz?

        Well if it's your business
      why are we all paying the price?
       sistahs listless in the night
      children can't read nor write

      Why would you sell our peace
        for a piece of their hell?
        unless you hate yourself
      and those who look like you

You gotta have it?
and just what is "it"?
if not shit
that won't be silent

     Like the shit that made you so defiant
        reliant on the same shit
      that make you so unreliable
            shit going on all over this world
                from sea to shining sea
                  shit is going down
                        shit
                that won't be silent

Our children are dying for shit
tired minds be lying for shit
and when shit is scarce
we be worrying for shit
        shit's getting bigger and stronger
        while creation dies from hunger
        so what is it with you and this shit?

    Was is not rolling around in shit
    in an unsuccessful effort to conceal the skin
        the spin
        that spawned
        unethical reforms
    like the paper currency concept
notes bearing false promises
like false witnesses
testifying at Mumia's trial?

Remember why money was called shit?
is that it?
is that what you're selling us out for?
or is that all you think you're worth?
        shhh!! shhh!!
        shit
        just won't be silent

Eat Shit and Die

Well into the twenty-first century
and we still eating pig feet
talking bout oh how so sweet
      we've been eating this shit for years
        the tail, the tongue even the god-damned ears
          we even eat the intestinal tract
            matter of fact
                we be eating pig shit
            some of us are starting to look like it

              They serve us this shit
           in the so-called house of the lord
         hearts heavy laden with lard and fat
we become vulnerable
to all matter of this and that
yet we say how sweet

         We marinate this shit
        we barbeque this shit
            we cure it bore it and pickle this shit
            death fingers our cells and sickles it
up goes our blood pressure
eating this shit has given us all manner of anemias
the enemy is in us
and surely sickness and death shall follow us
              as we
           eat shit and die

Know ThySelf

Your high mind that sits high
and looks low
seeking thru Ma'at
to influence the seeds you sow
this is the seat of your Tehuti
the first eye to see
what you can truly be
knowing that you will truly be
what you will to be
so know thyself
for your self
and love thyself
in spite of yourself

Fences and Rusty Nails

I see fences
fences of by-gone circumstances
repeating themselves as everyday occurrences
bordering the mind
the gateway to the imagination

Imagine Black men still swinging from trees
in this day and time

Imagine Black men on death rows
trumped up charges unlawful death sentences
I see fences

Fences half-mended at broken joints
held together ever so precariously
by rusty nails

Like the nails that pierced the flesh
of our messiahs
driven deep into hands that share
into hearts that care
rusty nails like bullets
making martyrs out of freedom fighters
rusty nails like unjust laws
keeping this system of injustice together
around us
like fences

Fences of dis-education
malnutrition
fences of mis-directed religions
pointing us in the wrong direction
away from the waters of life
I see fences
held together by rusty nails

Question It

                    We move thru thick white smoke
                                    inhaling the mist
never once asking from whence comes this
        believing that they got our best interest
                                              at heart

We dismiss notions of corporate conspiracies
that pharmaceutical companies
have invested billions
in genetically targeted dis-eases
that to them
we are still less than human
we say we are Americans
        citizens of this brave and so called free country
                where red white and blue flies freely
        symbolic of their white male non-supremacy

                But we be black
          living every day in the red
          some wishing they were white
          spending our days feeling blue

                    We move through thick white smoke
                              inhaling the mist
never once asking from whence come this
now the whole neighborhood is sick

Each Brother Matters

We used to be proud of each other
now we just get loud on each other
on the road to success
two is a crowd to each other
with peace signs and hugs
we bowed to each other
brotherly love showered on each other
to err is human was allowed of each other
our mission seems impossible
so each other dis-avow each other
as each other devour each other
who other than each other
got the back of each other?
we used to be proud of each other
now to each brother
each other
is no longer
each other's brother
so each brother
no longer matters
to each other

After-Thought

After the after-life what's next?
when checks and balances
are replaced by texts and sexual chances
who's perplexed?
who's vexed?
that carnal knowledge is taught in kindergarten
where minds are the kind of garden
where kinder thoughts play
too many children raising too many children
without the way
so too many children tend to stray
too many children not taught
to meditate and pray
so their bodies grow
but their minds don't know
the only word they know is 'so'
ignorant of the law that they'll reap what they sow
they don't know
that there's life after the after-life
the weighing of the heart dictates peace or strife
so where are your children being taught?
are they the results of your thoughts
or just an after-thought?

This Damned Nation

No,
it's not a jungle out there
and we're not animals to fear
for the jungle is a natural habit
where nature is the law
while this here damned nation
is where we be imprisoned at
where street soldiers are bred to war

No,
the Black in me
be not evolved from the ape
though we be conditioned to kill our likeness
bear false witness
then rape

This is psychological warfare of this damned nation
where they distort the truth
pollute the minds of our youth
commit psychological murder
against our god-nature

And who be the real mad scientists
commissioned to attack the black
but the soul predators
who reward sell-out artists
with self-defaming weapons of recording contracts
they seek only to profit
from the slaughter of our poets and prophets
replacing their scientific sights
with rented mics
some say Mcees
who spread the will of this damned nation
like rabies
you know them
the wanna bees
like mafia
how now brown cow
you be his junior
so he be your senior
your master
and like the fat cow
he means to devour the lean
for to him your ass is grass
seeking after his green
but the truth will set you ablaze
like fire
you retire
amazed
as rattle snakes creep for cover
from the lyrics of those scientific liars

For he who has the gold
cast a mean fly for the soul
hooking even the elect
who selects
the image of his god on paper
I pen now a sequel
to the gladiators arena
come now yesterday's Caesar
today's scientific liar

And this here ain't nothing
but his united snakes of political mayhem
where our minds are phucked up
phucked over
then flushed down his political sewage system
in this here his united laboratory
we be his guinea pigs
where his experiments
are considered a success
when we successfully
learn to express ourselves like animals
his animals
to be named and tamed like pets
come now snoopy the little doggy
fetch your bone your biscuit
tell me

how many brothers have you delivered
in a casket?
your master is pleased
when he sneezed
you wiped his nose
as you relegate our Black pearls
to bitches and hoes
now get along
run along
to your laid back crib
by the way
my baby sister got one of those

Cross-Over Poet

I remember
way, way back when
you first picked up the pen
and breathed prosaic life
back into the trees
you would say to me
I had a vision
and this is what I sees

I remember
how you would interrupt me
as I went about handling my affairs
and I would listen so patiently
to what you so eagerly shared

I watched you as you grew
I swore you knew
from whence came the energy

Perhaps it was your
invocation of the ancestors
your call for revolution
to brothers and sisters
your "give thanks to the creator"
creator of all things great and small
that led me to believe
you truly understood it all
but I was wrong wasn't I?

For to you
this poetry thing
was just a means to the end$
    a way out and into
   the coupes, the Lexxies and the Benz

      So you kissed all the right asses
       and have finally succeeded
        in being totally deceived
         as you believed
        it's all about you
         your words
        your thoughts
         your vibes
        your energy
     what a fool you turned out to be

For you couldn't feel a damned thing
if not for the melanin in your being

To this let me testify
that by and by
everything must change
for this revolution is inevitable
and you will be most regrettable
as you sit helplessly
     and watch your fame
      turn to shame.

For this revolution
will not be led by
sports gladiator superstars
their owners and sponsors
won't allow it
suspensions and fines
will threaten their
country club memberships
much like the gladiators of old
feared the whip.

Nor will this revolution
be led by popular recording artists
for it is our misery
that propel them to gold and platinum
        their narrow-minded ambition
        is simply to sell another album
        and who of you
        will ask them
        to distribute their assets
        isn't that why
        they kissed all the asses?

        And what of the cross-over poet
        will they re-cross the burning sand
        and re-join the effort to plug the leak
        stand with those who refuse
        to turn the other cheek
or will the sell-out thought continue
as Yurugu serves you tea
on the White-House lawn

as slaughtered souls cry out
and tortured minds mourn
cause you let Yurugu be

You say now
his world is a beautiful place
that with a little hard work
    we can all be free
    but that's a damned lie
    and you know it
    Poet
    or have you lost
    your taste for truth
        are your eyes now fixated
        on Yurugu's loot?

For his world is a goddamned disaster
and your massa's no master
but a master of lies and deception
        reception granted
        to those who please him

    I remember
    way, way back when
    you first picked up the pen
    and now
    you don't read for me
    any more

<u>The Low on Their High</u>

Hear my words warriors
         we come now trapped
        like Gilligan on his island
           in his mind
    where thoughts are full of play
        we say
      we are at home
               but they tell lies to our vision
                      with our eyes
               on their green prize
            we make ill decisions

We find ourselves displaced by time
like warriors in the mist
we seek to replace our minds
            we sift through the smokey fog
                 we smoke
          but without divine knowledge
              we can only choke
though there is an opening of the way
we do not go higher
      instead we come now dazed
      inspired by lustful desires

Daily we raise the estrogen in our system
making our subjugation easier for them
we become spiritually passive
and when revolution dawns
we sing
can't we all just
get along
as they prompt us to
move along

We are then like fattened cows
grazing in the fields of Yurugu's poisoned grass
brother to brother
we seek to surpass
with Cain and crack
we trap those less able
mentally shackled
we are led to yurugu's stable
be it his jail house
his slaughter-house
his white-house
their high
can take you very low

Shake Those Bones

Oh ye dry bones
you creep the streets at night
your lack of sight leads to your gravesite
you are restless
the rising sun reveals your comatose repose
languished in the anguish of your sorrows
deep in the valley of death
where you cry alone
Oh ye dry bones

Your bones are broken and lifeless
yet helpless
you help yourself to more of that American Pie
gulping the wine mashed from the grapes of wrath
laughing the laugh of the despised clone
Oh ye dry bones

How long lay you idle
while yurugu feeds your thoughts
thoughts that feeds the nightmares
nightmares that induces actions of the beast
yet you drink and make merry
in yurugu's feast?

How long will you shake your bones
to the unrighteous asynchronous beat
while yurugu taps his feet
all over your dry bones?

How long will you sentence to abandon
the children home alone in this land of damnation
while you slave your fingers to the dry bones?

Oh ye dry fragile Black bones
ye dope slinging
drive-bying
while your people be dying
Black dry bones
ye baby making
then forsaking
Black dry bones

Ye white women chasing
Black culture erasing
Black dry bones

Oh ye soap opera minded
gotta have a rich man
too cute to walk in the sun
wanna-bee European
Black dry bones

Ye overly materialistic
Black man makes you sick
can't cook and proud of it
must wear the latest design
half ass negro mind
Black dry bones

Will the darkness of ignorance and impotence
forever consume our minds
like a final sentence
do we not know the hour?
will we forever relinquish the power
to refind our minds?

Oh ye dry bones
ye Black dry bones
won't you shake up
and wake up
then make up
your minds?

The Season to Reason

Come
come with me
let us reason together
for the season of dying
has long since been gone
and the season of living awaits us

But yet do we fear
the ashes to ashes
the dust to dust
so we put our whole trust
in the not so prudent hands of Prudential
                              then consequential
we live our lives unto death
breath by painful lonely breath
we journey

Thru this dark and desolate valley
unable to tally
        the cost of our life long folly
    we sing "blessed assurance"
        while seeking life assurance
      for a life lived in total darkness

                    Our lives bear false witness
                       we lack spiritual fitness
                    to rescue our helpless youth
                      who like helpless lepers
                carry the plague of our ignorance
                        blind to the whole truth

So to these streets they creep
then like things that creep
            their confrontations become ritual
                they drop dead
                  one by one
          from complications that are spiritual
                  I say come
                 come with me

Tarry awhile with me in thought
for naught
we bend our knees at night and pray
and we pray
when all day
we cuss and fuss
and fuss and cuss
think we
this life be
a dress rehearsal
for some by and by?
should we
confess to sins
we shall not surely die?

surely we know
we reap what we sow
but so corrupt are the thoughts we were taught
that our children will sell
the same bullshit their fathers bought
so come
come with me

Let us reason together now
for the season of living
is upon us now
are we ready for life?

<u>Fear No More</u>

We were afraid once
ones and guns became our gods of choice
choosing to live the life of the victim
victory alluded us
taken again by the wind
we were afraid once

Inner-sight blighted by fear and frustration
willingly we rushed
into the arms of the beast for comfort
forgetting the sun will always come forth
homelessness and hopelessness loomed before us
like ignorance and impotence
we were afraid once

Now the days of strayfull ways are no more
to hell with yurugu we fear no more
like wolves baying at the moon
we yell no more
tales of defeat
we tell no more

We were afraid once
ones and guns became our gods of choice
now
we are the gods we choose to be

Grow The Children

These are the days of lost children
and found pets
the cost goes unpaid
as crosses are nailed
to the broken backs of dis-abled vets
checks are cashed
for another broken promise
notes are missed
as their plights we dismiss
empty lives we lead
yet we care not to know
who owes the piper
when our grass refuses to grow

        Who holds the keys to the lost rooms
where knowledge, understanding, and wisdom
                      orbit the same moon?
to whom shall the drummer's message be told
             when the old cannot be found
                    amongst the young
                          the strong?
             too weak to see their plight
        the night comes to soon for most
       they never had the chance to fight

empty lives we lead
yet we care not to know
who owes the piper
when our grass refuses to grow

The end comes and finds most sleeping
weeping the silent river
we long for the sea
where the days of bending
will no longer be
becoming one with the sun
we'll run the course of our destiny
we'll take to the sky
on the wings of air
the piper is paid in full
no more fear
as our children begin to grow

Saga of The Black Stone

There must be another world
besides this one
the one that gods so love
like that promise land prophets and poets spoke of
from whence the Afrikan fell and failed to rise above
trapped in his own matrix and would not come out of

Come now Afrikan black Stone to cast
into a world with no answers
only questions to ask
this is the world that mankind jacked
then forced the Afrikan to build
where seeds of the black stone
too soon became the belated
the dearly departed
black stone now the hated

So Jack who jacked the Black world refuses it
its name
it's language
it's culture
plants it on plantations
then sets about confusing it
                              Black stone finds a corner
                                  becomes chief in it
                      infinite possibilities revealed in it

There must be another world
without guns and bullets
for this one has no love for the law in stone
they eat their own
dead Presidents commands them from the grave
cornerstones to this world are the reservation brave
and the integrated slave

Declarations and treaties are political lies
they drop A-bombs day by day
count their money by night
as original people die
young people
old people
red, brown, and gold people
store keepers of the melanin
then they say to the false priests
"bless me father for I have sinned"
they go to church and pray
spawning the likes of Timothy McVeigh
while cries of the innocent
echoes from around the way
that's why I say
there must be another world

Where religious sell-outs find no sustenance
for they know not the hour nor the science
like finance is the way we love to feel
doctors really know how to heal
and when we kneel
it's out of respect for each other
like fathers supporting their babies
and the mothers
this is the world of the Black Stone
a world where one is never alone
this is the world we can call home
                                      the one that gods so love
                                          where we show love

<u>No Thanks</u>

And the children of the enslaved Afrikans joined the children of the European enslavers in giving thanks to the god of the enslavers for blessing the enslavers with victory in slaughtering, beheading, and enslaving the indigenous peoples of America, and for delivering the Afrikan unto them to be used and abused as property.

The children of the enslaved Afrikans will then willingly give their hard-earned money back to the children of the European enslavers on a day known as 'Black Friday'. This is when the children of the European enslavers take stock of just how many of the children of the enslaved Afrikan still belong to them, body, mind, and soul as they the enslavers children join together in a chorus and sing praises unto their god 'chi-ching, chi-ching, oh sweet chi-ching, don't ever wake our niggers keep them sleeping, chi-ching oh sweet chi-ching, let them struggle to pay their bills while we go ski-ing, oh sweet chi-ching'.

Shades of View

As the poet dreams
it seems a dream dreamt
to the beat of the heartland drum
the beat that meets the mind
in the melting pot of thought and reality

Dreams of drums beating
in the deep blackness
the beat that meets the moon
greets the moon
the beat that whispers sweet nothings to the stars
and forms words in the lightness of sound

Words heard by many
discerned by few
a chosen few
those in need of its honey-dipped
vinegar-based messages
chanted, screamed, whispered, hummed
in shades of view
to those who have eyes and see not
the poet sees the unseen
then pens a scene
that stirs to consciousness
the collective consciousness of a people

As the poet releases the flood gate
to the gate-way of the inner self
thoughts original but familiar
to those who were before
rushes down the highway of the imagination
flooding the mind with a consciousness
whose time has come

Suddenly
without knowing
the poet knows the path of the unknown
knows of stories left untold

As the poet loves the trees with the pen
one hears song birds melodiously enchanting
mountains bow their heads
in reverence to the eagle flying high
drawing nigh to its crown
                    as the poet is born
                    shades of view
                    come into view
                    fade then to you

Dues to Love

There are those
whom I have made
into someone special
then I have laid
but seldom long
have I stayed
around long enough
to have paid
my dues
to love

Pledge of Allegiance

And so
with pride aside I come
I come to you proudly
said this king to his queen
I love you loudly

I am yours forever from this day
as we unite together come what may
our hearts gladly sing the praise
as darker nights bring brighter days

Let's leave behind our sad memories
take our time on this journey oh darling please
let me be the only one for you
show you love tried and true

Though I am stripped of my ancestors riches
and am unworthy of your gaze
I vow to love you always
deserving of the rest of your days
so come

Go with me to an Afrikan paradise
where the trees are tall
and everything's nice
I'll trim the grass under your feet
and give you my heart
with every beat.

Passion in the Night

                      With a twist in your hips
                   you bring the night to my day
                   with a moistness on your lips
              you sing the words I want to say

I saw visions of passion between the sheets
as our spirits danced together
our bodies in heat
            endless was that moment
              I held you tight
                        relentlessly pursuing
                         that feeling so right

            Inside of me
       my manhood moved strong
as we danced the night away
            to the love song
                     I know you felt it too
               as you matched my rhythm
          pressing your body real close
                against what had arisen

          I felt your desire
       burn like a red hot fire
as the temperature of our passion
    climbed higher and higher

For now the moment has ended
and the day returns
the night is gone
but the memory lives on

In my heart I knew
that you were the one
to bring the night to my day
and perhaps
a song.

Let us Be

Special thoughts
and special feelings
the seasons belong to you
and to me
those thoughts that are most revealing
are the ones of your infinite beauty

A beauty that's deeper than the deepest ocean
a beauty wider than the widest horizon
it seems always to be in motion
and never stops to ask the reasons

Why is there always a magic in the air
whenever you are far or near?
why is there something about the way you are
that makes me wanna wish upon a star?
to make you shine your desire on me
and let be what must be

Our hearts are ready
both you and I
to be lovers
let's give it a try

Body Parts to Body Bags

We lead each other by golden chains
mis-leading each other time and time again
like dogs in heat
we roam the streets
looking for fresh meat
sniffing out body parts
judging each other to be whole
based on emotional starts

He didn't marry her mind
he married her ass
he married every man
she ever slept with
he married her past
no love in the mix
he gives her his heart
naïve to love she takes it
spiritually un-evolved she breaks it
now emotionally involved they fake it

As he moans she screams
nightmares and bad dreams
he tries to shake himself awake
but he's spilled too much precious seed
all for the sake of pleasure
now he spiritually bleeds
no more stored up treasure

He lacks then that spiritual energy
that life force
our soul source
unable to enter that spiritual womb
he fails to be born again
as they take him away
in a body bag.

When Doves Cry

It was not for you that I wept
but for the love I grew for you
and knew
that as surely as time passes
so will this too

                              It was not for you that I wept
                        but for the love that saw less of you
                           and more of its impending death
                          more of the approaching stranger
                  bearing a bright smile and a promise
            bringing with him the end of our beginning

With glossed over impressions
deep committed cunning
he carried your heart away
to a land of part time bliss

                                        I wept inwardly
                               the tears broke thru
                            the walls of my heart
                                   finding a path
                      to the windows of my soul
                           so I wept outwardly
                              I wept openly
                            it was not for you
                        but for the pain I felt
                            at losing our love

A Parting of Ways

            The part that makes me want to cry
                is in the days that lay ahead
              from beyond the tears I shed
               for you never gave us a try

        The Part that makes me want to sing
          belongs to my strong input of love
         being ever so real as the sky above
              we were just beginning

The part that makes me want to die
develops as today becomes yesterday
my love has been cast astray
you never even said good-bye

        The part that makes me want to befriend
          someone more worthy of my love
                      all the pain now resolved
                          my thoughts of you
                              are at an end.

Days of Our Lives

                                          Who can separate
                                the arrow from the quiver
                                    as the bow is drawn
                                          the sun dawns
                                  rays of hope to deliver

                The sun finds us seeking lifestyles
                    rich enough to ruin the liver
                            tuning into soaps
                      to wash our brains with

These be the days of our lives
where the young Black man leaves home
                        seeking golds on the streets of war
                              then sees home no more

These be the days of our lives
where warriors are slain
before they're born
                where sleepers must come awake
                      with the dawn
            and keepers of secrets become
                    teachers of one

There's More

Deep deep down inside the youth
Stirs a guest at best for the truth
there burns the fires of war
then there's more

                                        Listen to the songs
                                   of their redemption
                                        their revolution
                                  a revelation of pain
                                          and pollution
                                      Black leaders guilty
                                  of political collusion
                           mixed messages produce
                                        mass confusion
                            intrusion is not inclusion
                                                hear me

absent of true cultural guidance they flee
they run from this imprisoning hypocrisy
on which this imposing democracy
whose true face is white male non-supremacy
states and stakes its claim
is maintained
not with symbiotic self-sacrifice
but with murder plunder and lies
as cries from mothers land is drowned
in spilled Afrikan blood
then there's more

They fall victims to sentences handed down
by clowns wearing gowns
lacking true tried wisdom
no repentance is sought
naught but a hardening of the heart
hear now a truth

The youth are mad sad and lost
without a clue
they seek to undo
they seek to know
they seek to grow
but there's no one to show
the way

So anger and hate dominate
dis-relate them from the straight
the road that's narrow
and leads back home

not to the Eastside
Westside
and all the other sides
but to the land that time has set aside
where cultural consciousness grows
spiritual consciousness flows
and "if I ruled my world" is reality
then there's more

The youth are angry
angry at our bad decisions
our lust for racial integration
while lost and turned out
                in our interpersonal cultural relations
                for us success is measured by
                how many things whitey do
                we can do too
                like
                drinking the poisoned waters that flow
                from their stolen golden fountains
                like
                eating his seven day-old road kill
                barbecued and salted to taste
                served up with a glass of sour grapes
                in his fancy red-carpet restaurant
                like
                breaking our backs
                borrowing from his banks
                promises promised
                against promissory notes
        used to buy pseudo-degrees
        signed by professional patients
        with mental diseases
        which gives us the right
        to go to work for him
in his greedy corporate system
where we exchange our pure energy
for stacks of green backed promises
that we promise to repay forever
        the youth see our hypocrisy
        as they wonder
        what ever happened to
        "neither a lender nor a borrower be"

The youth are angry at our impotence
our lack of common-sense
our inability to guide them
to provide them
with the knowledge of who they are

Angry because we refuse to recognize
the devil that lies
behind the eyes
the fake smiles of some of these world-leaders
these here corporate plantation holders
who like the piper that pied
leads us to our doom
our gravesite
then there's more

The youth feel alone and confused
so they seek to live hard fast then die
so into the streets they spill
as they fill
the prison industrial complex food chain
and before most are born to knowledge
they're slain
yet others pledge their lives to unholy armed forces
come now bearers of guns
abandoned sons
then die for lost causes

       Let the elders rise up
       still the spill of black blood
      black hearts filled with gloom
let us teach them how to destroy and whom
let them destroy this hypocrisy
this self-contained complacency
let them destroy white male non-supremacy
     with an empowered will to be
     all that they were meant to be

Math of the 2 Pillars

You're no gangster
captain crunching your bowl of cheerios
in stereos
you're just a cereal-killer
your name ain't no lil' this or young that
your last name is Miller
so if you study your history
you'll know we been thru one hell of a thriller
we been grilled, guts spilled
then skinned like the chilliest chinchilla
so you ain't saying nothing but empty fillers
while you pocketing change they the master billers
but you can change all that
if you master the math of the 2 pillars
instead of renting a mic to kill your brother
use that Afrikan might to build with your brother
then you and your brother rise to the top together
generations later generations still at the top together
all because you dared to see the bigger picture
your last name was really never Miller.

I Grow Weary Sometimes

I grow weary sometimes
and sometimes I worry how times
just seem to be getting harder
our lack of functional unity
make each burden heavier
crosses and mountains we leave as legacies
like leaves falling from the trees
can the son be greater than the father?
I grow weary sometimes
and sometimes I worry how times
just seem to be getting harder

The ancients have said
joy comes in the morning
but many mornings come
many mornings go
most have found me mourning

Mourning with sac-cloth and ashes for deliverance
mourning for hearts heavy with repentance
mourning for those who cry in the night
and for those who refuse to
mourning for lives filled with strife
for those who are refused too

mourning for the fathers and mothers
who refuse to be Kings and Queens
but instead make separate beds
as unto the ways of independence
passing their days like a final sentence
I grow weary sometimes
and sometimes I worry how times
just seem to be getting harder

While the earth quakes
mountain shakes
heart aches
for we the originals grow more perverse
in our ways
some say diverse and alternate lifestyles
but ponder awhile
                who carries the womb?
of whom shall we be ashamed?
if not us then who's to blame?
where is the village that raises the children?
I grow weary sometimes
and sometimes I worry how times
just seem to be getting harder

We Be Angels

Dearly beloved
by the power of the ancients vested in we
tested in me
I now pronounce to you
I announce to you
that sometimes
sometimes we be angels

Let those who entertain be aware
that they entertain us unaware
with spoken words we step to fears
mending broken souls vanquishing nightmares
for sometimes
sometimes we be angels

                         Rising wingless against the night
                              our spirits take flight
                                 on words of power
                              we be the rising sons
                                like chosen ones
                                    we choose
                              like those who chose
                                    parting seas
                                 scaling degrees
                                    for sometimes
                            sometimes we be angels

We be angels of Life
angels unto death
our breath be words
that keep warriors from falling
seal the book
before our doom come calling

Like bridges over troubled water
we close the gaps in the mind
drawing maps to the dawn of time
for therein was the word
and so were we
where seeds of thought fertilized her power
powerful words then born
let there be light
worlds were formed
and in that moment we knew
that sometimes
sometimes we be angels

The Greatest of These

Day by day we slip
night by night we trip
hip hop down on uncharted roads of Life
without third eye sight
falling

In and out of pot-hole circumstances
chances we take
with unlawful romances
responses from "feel so good" emotions
establishing devotions
that leads to lifelong imbalances
drinking from the cup of bitter regrets
we wish for second chances
day by day

Night by night
our heartbeats quicken
keeping time to a corrupted rhythm
our breath goes shallow
once seekers of divinity
now pimped like hoes
thru starring roles
welfare lines
and sacrificial hip hop videos

who rescues the fallen sparrows
that fall far from graceful trees?
when we tease gods-to-bees
with sneak peaks and back door glances
now with the wolves we dances
crawling on hands and knees
for those who betray us daily
dearly beloved

Day by day we slip
down treacherous roads in this world
without third eye sight
heartbreaks wakes us from sleepless nights
we fall hard from spiritual heights
lights go out
as we plunge into the abyss
dreams shattered
schemes and games no longer matter
we blame our shame on love
but what does love got to do with this?
when we dismiss Ma'at
divine law divine truth
since the days of youth
I say
day by day we slip

Night by night we trip
over inflated egos
where it goes
our hearts are sure to follow

for this is all we know
descending our mountains of rationalizations
with half spoken words and filled in blanks
spilling ego-soothing interpretation
on the science of giving thanks
killing each other softly
with songs that blind third eye
hoping to sleep through the storm that shatters the lie
too late
our hearts have been compromised
the pain of falling egos stains our pillows
we blame our shame on love
with the greatest of ease
now we cry with the doves
as we come now the least
for the greatest of these
is love

The Way of the Soul

                                    Be still my soul
                            trouble don't last always
                   ways to brighter days unfold daily
                              our dearly departeds
                            have not departed us
                                they be part of us
                                part of our souls
                                        be still

This passageway where sages passed
past pains transformed
into brilliant roads of energies
this passageway that joins us all
binds us all
this is the way of the soul
the way of the sages
be still

                    And if this be the way of the soul
                             then the soul is love
              for love is the tie that binds us all
                          that demands of us all
                that each one must teach one
                          that each one is soul
                              each one is love
                                  and loved
                                        be still

I Speak of Ma'at

                    We fear to draw near
             to each other we show fear
          for lack of trust and self-hate
                has us unable to relate
but who binds us but ourselves?
it is I and I who must bear the blame
it is I and I who causes her to act in shame
it is I and I who must say
        to hell with poppin' games
     it is I and I who must once more
          look to the law
for the law is perfect in its design
to hell with mankind's law
I speak of the divine
             the same law that keeps the sun
        from wandering about aimlessly in the sky
            I speak of Ma'at

Questions of the Time

This poem is designed
to stimulate your mind
not just with the elements of rhyme
but with questions of our time

And let not these questions
prove too hard to ponder
for I wonder

How long dare we sleep
the deep sleep of the beguiled
while the bastards ruin the Nile
the deep sleep of the bewitched
are we proud of sleeping with the devils bitch?

Dogged by a klan of cavemen
now we dog each other
for a chance to sit
at the front of his bus
we fuss and cuss each other
with the tongue of the demon nigger
possessed of this demon
struggling to be bigger
bigger than brother
bigger than sister
we come now bigger the nigger be bitter
so

Can peace without
be found without
peace within?
the soul that is
not just the skin

And is the skin the thing
that makes a man
a god-conscious man
a brother-man?

Come now,
does how we wear our hair
dreaded, froed, or bare
define our character?

Did or does the second skin
as in fashion statement
protect any of the kings
from assassination
or arraignment?

When daggers of hate are launched
from the mind of greed
who bleeds?
are mixed breeds any less qualified
to suffer and endure
the slings and arrows of outrageous fortune hunters?

How long will we glory in their possessions
that possesses our souls?
per chance to sit at the devil's table
we deny kinship to the whole
we gaze into their "look so rich" bowl of soup
soup made of the flesh of a thousand slain warriors
seasoned with the crowns of our forgotten she-roes
we long for their freedom

But what is freedom without truth?
who selected these sell-out leaders to office
where they continually deliver us
for thirty pieces of silver and a Lexus
whose sole purpose is to entrap our souls
in a web of deception?
did they not define our freedom as integration
into a degenerate system
from which no good fruits can come?

What of this obsessive obsession
with their freedom?
when will we cease this
spiritual masturbation?
that fills our egos to bursting
stop this pre-mature ejaculation
of our soul-source
that leaves our life force
weak and ripe like game
and while we seek the fame
of the devil's name
our women and children
run the streets like beasts
for the cavemen in blue to tame

              Has 'free the people'
                      like 'peace'
              become mere buzzwords
                   like passwords
      that allows our enemy into our midst?
             the enemy that looks like us
                       talks like us
                       walks like us
                       and like us
                        dis-like us
              then walks all over us

Will the spirits who were before
who built the pyramids out of wilderness
formulated mathematics without the stress
scaled degrees unlike their B.S.
forsake us now
in the hour of our greatest need
the need to functionally unite
quit this Black on Black fight
and love each other
with all our might?

              What man can find the spirit
                  and bind the spirit
              when ashes turns to ashes
                  and dust becomes dust
              are we not our spirits free?

Then what is this freedom that we die for
that we buy for
that we sell our souls
and each other's for?

Will we take the time
to ponder on
these questions of our time?

The Winds of Change

We hear not
we fear not
the burning spear
we care not to do right
only that we feel right
feeding our animal instincts
we think
just one more drink
we be knee-deep in our bullshit
distinctively unreal
as we deal each other spiritual death blows
let the winds of change blow

Just as wild horses came tame to the whip
then around the tract they go
we take a deadly mind trip
along the path of self-defamation
in that race for lifestyles of the loveless
in this we are not blameless
to our children's angry and confused mindsets
we offer no solutions
merely blowing up and getting large
on the up-chuck from emcee Fed
that master criminal
that red necked bastard
whose stars and stripes
continuously strips our families apart

while patching the frame work with political pitchforks
packed with a false sense of social security
economical enslavement enhanced
by a lack of god-knowledge
I say
turn up the winds of change.

Against the Law

Who blows the wind and calls the seas to be?
riding the rhythm of the waves
to bring the sands of time to shore
this I saw
that even the very drops of rain
fall according to the Law

And in this here world of artificial intelligence
where sacrificial lambs are offered
to satisfy the superficial rich and famous
broadcast commercials of the armed and dangerous
where much sought after physical elegance
typically suppresses spiritual relevance
it's against the law
to ignore the Spirit

For what is matter void of consciousness
but an empty shell of what will never be
a shadow of a doubt that can never see
a reflection of past time
cast thine against troubled waters
then tell me
what really matters

When by-pass is performed against the soul
you and I now no longer whole
come now a fraction of I and I
and by and by
we pray
that the sins of our forefathers
be fully paid for
it's against the law
to ignore the spirit

And who forms the clouds
cracks the thunder aloud?
who moves with lightening across the sky
and gives the eagle her wings to fly?
this I saw
that even the sunrays are obedient to the law

But come now man's kind
with a different agenda
to confuse the genders
woe but for the law of ions
we would all be blinded by his illusions
confusions wrapped in true confessions
that mimics the created reality
come now virtual reality
but where now is the electricity?
when positive takes positive to bed
wrapped in the romance of the dead
where now is the electricity?
minds no longer grounded
seek then to defy gravity

When negative meets negative
behind white clouds
can the blind lead the blind?
can the weak bear the burden of the weak?
who dares then to fool with mother nature
                        when all that is of the earth
                        returns to her sooner or later
                                  I tell you
                            it's against the Law
                that one man should seek another
                        this I saw
           that even judgement will be judged
              according to the Law of Ma'at.

<u>Here I Am</u>

I am one ray of the morning sun
ascending from the East with the dawning
with each ascension my soul is reborning
re-emerging from the ashes like phoenix rising
seeking to inherit the earth
my earth-right

To bathe her
in the beauty of the light
to purge her
the sins of her poison fruits
the frightened youths
who look to the West for salvation
but damnation is all they reap
while mothers weep
for those who go too soon
into the night

I am possessed of the living light
descendant of the fullest moon
a beam in the night
sent to redeem
the blood of our ancestors
like the tide that rises
ascension awaits us

                    Thru the eye of the storm
                    I brings the rage in the night
              enemies overcome with full moon madness
                         see them now
                       like a herd of swines
                   they rush over the precipice

I am the voice crying shame
descending mountains
walking thru flames
bringing spoken words of love and hate
                    hope and doom
                    peace and war
                     life and death
                  I am a thought-shifter
                   consciousness lifter
                        here I am

Show Me

As I journey from the depths of the valley
where our dry bones refuse to stir
    from the trenches of these besieged homelands
        where the blood of the innocent
        is likened unto a familiar drink
        take me to the highest mountaintop
            and show me

        Show me the promise land
        where little black boys
        play with little black girls
        and no one is dying

Show me a black father
with a black mother
loving and raising
a little black baby
and no one is crying

Show me a people
governed by a righteous government
elected by the right-for-us in mind
and no one is lying

Show me a village
that raises it's children
where the wisdom of the elderly spirit
is drawn upon like an eternal well
that never runs dry

Show me a time
where are no more drive-bys
Show me the way
to show us the way
back home

Thru the Valleys

Yay
though we walk thru the valley
this valley here
then that valley there
we tally the cost
of all who are lost
we see devils grinning
with no remorse
brothers killing brothers
to be endorsed
others willing to ride that white horse
and we wonder
will we ever make it home
or will we languish forever alone
in this here valley of dry bones

This here Amerikkka
home to the reservation brave
and the integrated slave
land of ill opportunities
false promises
broken treaties
where judges robes hide
the true color of look-black Thomasses

Where Black mothers sweet dreams
form dream teams
seeking gold
and concentration nursing homes
are prepared for those who grow old
Yay

Though we walk thru the valley
where snakes and states unite to attack
those melanated descendants of the perfect Black
where they continuously plague us
with lifestyles of the bitch who named us
where Afrika's stolen treasures
are used up then discarded
gifts of love retarded
where politicians polish their lull-la-lies
then go to speaking
white men lose control of black balls
then go streaking
the truth exposed
shake the sleep of the comatosed
we hear their cries
they sense their woes

So they go to raising Cain
to slay those who are able
passing laws
like rumors of wars
soon comes the day
when we turn the tables
Yay

Though we walk thru this valley
we walk not alone
we hear the lamentations of other warriors
warriors that be brothers
warriors that be sisters
calling all to reason together now
for as surely as the season turns
our enemies will burn
let your pain be my pain
let us join our voices and say never again
shed your tears
and so shed your fears
let us know courage
in these times where right seems wrong
let the weak seek the company of the strong
for it is weeping time no more
but reaping time now
and the destiny of the doers of bad deeds
the sowers of ill seeds
is likened unto a bundle of dry weeds

Though we walk now thru this valley
soon comes the hour
when all our valleys will be traveled
all mysteries unraveled
we pray and we pray
heavenly mother show us the way
for yay
though we walk thru the valley of this dam-nation
we will fear no evil.

Sour or Sweet

We don't hardly speak
all we do is text and tweet
our eyes never meet
don't know if we trick or treat
FaceBook got us looking neat
but in person are we sour or sweet
sour or sweet
sour or sweet
we don't hardly speak

The Blood

For hope is an eternal spring
from which our fore-fathers fathers did drink
passing it down thru the blood
while blood banks are formed
under banner of red crosses
I tally our losses

As crippled minds
spill the bloods of their brothers
man-made diseases
corrupt the bloods of others
our enemies surely know
that our hope is in our blood
so why don't we?

<u>These Times Test Us</u>

              I say now to the best of them
       and pray now with the rest of them
                 that we may now be strong
                  in these times that test us
                        I say thus

                      That these be trying times now
                          and lying minds be seeking
                              but to be using us
                                then loosing us
                          like good cop bad cop
                          they be confusing us
                              choosing us
       as carriers of their flameless torches
          bearers of their unholy crosses

We who are the greatest
now publicly displayed
as the weakest
for all the world to see
to hell with their publicity
their Oscars and their Grammys
these be trying times now
and they be wooing our hungry souls
with glimmer and glamor
yet do we clamor
to be party to their pagan mind-trip
there false god worship

                    Yet do we sleep with dogs
                        only to rise with fleas
                     then flee from our children
scratching the tic toc of the clock
from our minds
for surely these be trying times

                    Where worshipers of the end$
                         justify their means
                      though it was not necessary
                    shedding their melanin
                    like a snake sheds its skin
                    forming unholy alliances
                       with the Shatan
who promises to reward them
with long since dead presidents

                    I say now to the best of them
                     these be trying times now
                        where drug dealing
                        human trafficking
                 multimillionaires continue to be made
                       while the righteous in mind
                       are untimely laid to rest
where they free those guilty of murder
while the innocent
who oppose their unjust ways
see no more free days
            I say now to our prisoners of war
               our political prisoners
            be strong in these times that test us
               I say thus
            these surely be trying times now

pg. 158

The state of our Black future is in jeopardy
these corporate American States have custody
rhapsody of the endangered
but not speechless young Black souls
who go into the night
but not quietly
kicking and hip hopping
they gang bang their way
into six degrees of excavation
                                    home now to the bosom
                                          of mother earth
                                        some find no peace
                                    for they cursed their birth

                        I say now to the best of them
                let us fight now for our young minds
              who seek not to be strong in these times
          but to be as wrong as their cultural crimes
let us fight now for our earth-right
our right to inherit the earth
                I pray now with the rest of them
                and say now to the best of them
                      if not now
                      then when?

Pure Yang

Though it lends itself to the physical world, its origin is of the spirit. It is pure and unrefined in its qualifications. It is energy that can be likened unto a kettle of boiling water, that bubbles from within and steams from without. This energy must be provided a path of its own and nothing must stand in its way, for as the wild mustang thunders towards its destination, so too must this energy be allowed to run its course.

Pure yang is destructive and loud. It is inconsiderate to the untrained. To those who are born again and again pure yang destroys to rebuild, it increases audibility so that silence may be appreciated. It exudes selfishness and inconsideration, so that a natural flow to selflessness and kindness to others may be enhanced. Pure yang is the fire that burns away the impurity, revealing the beauty of the inner being.

Without this force of yang, the soft does not exist. There is a time of "yin", after the "yang". Just as the quiet chirping of the sparrows follows a raging storm.

Warrior or Soldier?

A warrior is spiritually strong
wages war against the wrong to right the wrongs
A warrior is mentally brave
walks like Harriett freeing the enslaved
perfects the cultural ways
instructs the youth of tried and tested truths
protects and respects the elders and queens
by any means
necessary

                              A soldier done sold his soul
                for a street corner and promise of gold
                                  he kills without shame
                                  lost in the loaded game
                              seeking fortunes and fame
                                    he makes a name
                                    amongst the lame
                                hip hop two three four
                       what the hell you fighting for?

                                  The motherland burns
                                    our ancestors turn
                     onward you Christian soldiers
                              marching us to war
                                    swallowing lies
                                    bellowing cries
                              as the rainforest dies

Dropping bombs night and day
then Presidents go to church and pray
now dead presidents
fought for night and day
you march to a strange drummer's beat
he owns your very feet
strips your mind of cultural melanin
your gun is pointed at your next of kin
soldier

Be a warrior
be free
wake up and be
warriors of Life

                                                    but not to be
                                                  soldiers of death
                      choose this day

<u>We Were One</u>

                                      Once we were one
                like many verses to the same song
                        our voices were strong
         few were there of the things we wanted
                 for we chanted together much
                                    and as such
        we supported the dream of each other
               brothers beholding unto brothers
                         as brothers should
                            we understood
                   the laws of our nature
         and walked upright in the way

Once we were one
We were men of wisdom
we showed ourselves approved
far removed
from the beast in us
we were in charge of our destiny
our storehouses grew large with currency
the profits of our cultural ways
our days welcomed the rising sun
our nights received the moon in peace

                    Now we are many
                 singing strange verses
                 to every and any song
                 something is very wrong
                    we have strayed far
                 far from the perfect path
                          our wrath
                we visit on each other daily
                    we are at war within
              and are too damned blind to see
             we have lost our universal rhythm

No longer do we chant for our needs
we take chances with our seeds
we march to the beat of a different drummer
from a distance we avoid each other
we fear to draw near
for lack of trust
but who binds us?
but ourselves

                         Once we were one
                      now we must once more
                          look to the law
                 for the law is perfect in its design
                        I speak of the Divine
                the same law that regulates the sun

the same law that has apportioned to each
its own space and time
this is not mine
this is divine law
this Law cannot be broken
for when the word was spoken
sequences unfolded
and from this law we were molded

            Once we were one with this law
              not we're at war with this law
                  but how can we win?
                we sow seeds of destruction
            then beg forgiveness for our sins
                    for how now we suffer
can any weapon formed against this law prosper?
how can you fool the mother of our nature?
when even the thought that we will think
she knows
this is how it goes

            We care not to do right
            only that we feel right
              but I say unto you
              check your emotions
         before you wreck your devotions
for though we have the freedom to choose
      we have not the right to choose
          that which leads us astray
              once we were one
          now we are as many fools

Tangled Web

Oh
what a tangled web we weave
we leave
our inheritance buried in the past
we cast
no reflection on those who went before
we worship
the image of false gods on paper
our souls are sold then dissipated like vapor
oh
what a tangled web

Weaving through our lives from every angle
we dangle like flies and super-flies
from alternate life styles
filled with lies
co-intel spies
and like the fish swimming in the sea
we cannot see
the net we enter
oh how entangled

As star spangled banners
are draped over our youth
the truth we avoid
we do not wish to be free
for truly we relish this life of poverty

for the spider has sat down beside us
has hypnotized us
has turned us one against another
brother against brother
sister against sister
mother against father
we would rather be slaves
rather than behave
like kings and queens
oh, oh
what a tangled web we weave

We dream of their "look-so-good" lifestyle
while they feed on our memories of the Nile
the spider means to own us
studying our genetics
it means to clone us
to make us over into their image
so they can control us

This is a smart spider
this spider seems friendly
but behind its red, white, and blue eyes
this spider is deadly
oh, oh, oh
this tangled web has been well woven
and we the chosen are the catch of the day

We Badly Pray

Let us pray
before we lay
lay we down to sleep
then we creep
creep on our knees
in the fashion of tradition
to our secret
not so secret closets
we go
seeking comfort of a god
we think we know
one by one
now that the day is done
and we pray
and we pray

Powerless words
words that lack the power
the power to move minds
in our habit we repeat lines
we repent lies
lies rehearsed
lines committed to memory since childhood
and after we've acted so badly
we badly pray to be good

We pray to someone's lord
to come now our souls to keep
yet our loved ones weep

they weep when we die
reluctantly relinquishing our souls
who sold us this lie of a by and by?
we do not believe
the very words we cry
but how can we
when we close third eye
then eyes have we
yet we cannot see
we do not seek
we hesitate
for to see within
is to meditate
instead we speak aloud
for to see without
is to hallucinate
and without a doubt
our words echo
thru the valleys they go
empty and powerless

The mountain still looms before us
threatening to erupt and corrupt our lives
yet do we lift
we lift our voices to the sky
we pray and we pray
heavenly father who art in heaven
but where does the sky end
and heaven begins?
how can we find the kingdom of God within
if we continue to pray
without
meditation?

Are we Romans yet?

Oh but for our mis-conceptions
like mal-nutritioned embryonic solutions
sired by the hypocrisy of mis-education
producing ambitions of mis-direction
erections of false gods
that demand our souls ejaculation

We come now like legal abortions
swinging from burning crosses
by that ill-umbilical biblical connection
that has us grateful
for their damned political contributions
which contributes to our mis-perceptions
deceptions distinguished as truths
the whole truth
and nothing but
oh but

Was in for naught
our ancestors fought
against the onslaught
of that beast from the north?
was it for naught our blood was shed?
and when the dead buries the dead
who lives to yell
"Lazarus come forth"?

Awake from this valley of dry bones
re-claim your earth right
to hell with their civil rights
let your suns rule by day
and your moons by night
oh but

For our mis-conceptions
our imperfections
infections of the blood
that leads to spiritual complications
struggling daily for social integrations
ignoring the stars we seek to become them
the children see the truth
so they take to the streets
with fatal thoughts of mayhem
and by far
who we were is not who we are
we come then like clones
like well-dressed bastards without a home
playing games in this land of damnation
ball games, mind games, war games
they're all the same
for games are but a time out
from reality

Our lives we measure by points and goals
another soul lost and turned out
come Sunday morning we jump and shout
yet

For the children born to death who weeps
when like fools we sleep
and we sleep
and we slip
deeper into that coma
where dreams of lies
are televised to the dreamer
replacing Ancestral warnings
with schemes of the schemer
oh but for our mis-conceptions

Our spiritual de-sensation
we come now senseless
we feel no pain
we cast no shadow
and without shame
we lead our enemies to the sight of our sorrow
who stands then in the door?
this gaping mocking hole in time
like this hole in our collective mind
where once held image of a beauty so real
we called her Alkebulan
who stands then in this door of no return?
this gaping mocking whole in time
like this hole in our mind
where thoughts once formed substance
from mathematical computations
now children are born to one without the other
we form no foundations
oh but for our mis-conceptions
are we Romans yet?

<u>Tweet this</u>

To save our youths from the streets
we gonna have to speak truth to the streets
not just beats on nets where we compete
           who got the most hits
           who got the most tweets

Your point-of-view may get the most views
your beat-backed spit may get the most hits
but the streets are decaying
them corners smell like shit
                        take them tracks off YouTube
                        take them to the corners
                        where young borners
                        come like goners
                        and languish
                        struggling with the Queens language
                        little hope in sight
                        they feel nothing but anguish

                        So minds and pants get to sagging
                        subliminal programs got some fagging
                        but before tongues get to wagging
                        let check-out clerks get to bagging
                        homo is a no-no
                        best left tween so and so
                        po-po kicks in front door
                        grandma cock glucks and fire

for a warrior's spirit never dies
never retires
but such an elder deserves
the protection of the young sons
where were the young ones?
the strong tongues
trapped on corners patrolled by stun guns
trigger fingers twitch with ill-intentions
now you sing sorry Ms Johnson
I need you to pay attention

Army bases converted to camps of concentration
what they got in mind for our young is incarceration
them streets are like Palestinian mine fields
young minds filled with mental fast-foods
labs produce thoughts that induce ill-moods
they back Black youths into street corners
most know before eighteen they're goners
so they march to the bass of Reagan's gangster rap
enter freebase the crack a CIA sponsored trap
add tough times, no jobs, no schools
watch them rush to death like fools
enter prison pipeline to be used as tools
no-knock warrants unleash blue forces
knock you upside your head no remorses
then court systems add one more to your losses
they got you in cross-hairs you soon to be corpses

To save our future from the streets
we need more than beats and tweets
we gotta speak truth to the youth
while we coining hashtags
they stacking body bags
these Black stars don't feel our pain
they feel only jet-lag
you and I gotta be the grass and the roots
we gotta tell our youths the truth
that the earth they're spilling their blood on
is actually their inheritance.

Ye be Gods

Goddesses come now to recharge a god
without charging a god
this is the hour of the changing of the guards
she does not engage in shaming a god
she knows there are no flaming gods
she's not into blaming gods
with each new birth she's re-naming gods
re-claiming gods
while mere mortals are gaming gods
she's untaming gods

Now for those who question
the relevance to culture
let me remind you
of ancient scriptures
know ye not that ye be gods?
now rise up you mighty Nubian gods
protect the womb of men
this is the hour of the charging of the gods
goddesses need the gods
to stand up and be the gods
for truly ye be gods
and if you truly be gods
then you will protect the womb of men
by any means necessary

Sooner or Later

I went looking for sooner
avoiding the wiley ways of later
you know
the other half that sits on this shoulder
whispers in this ear
to do that shit later
but where does sooner end
and later begins?

Me, Myself, and I

I sit in my dark room and develop myself
I expose myself to myself
showing myself who's inside myself
I see myself for myself but not by myself
I am myself
like double exposure
I am me myself and I
that means I am we
for we and I are one
and that is the meaning of love
like the man in the mirror
it all begins with
me, myself, and I

This is for the Birds

They tell you to kill two birds with one stone
before you wash your hands
they send you to kill the mockingbird
when you ask them why
they stick their middle finger in your eye
and they shoot you the bird
you come now like a bird in hand
they using you to lure two more out the bush
you hear a caged bird crying in the background
they tell you it's singing
the ghetto filled with cuckoo birds trying to rest
helicopters flying over its nest
now they have all the ducks in a row
while the rest of us eating crow
here comes Jim Crow…again

People of the Bus

We've been in this land far far too long now
gotten on and off damn near every bus in town now
bussing here, bussing there
then cussing each other
like we just don't care
fussing bout our sneaks, tees, and horse tail hair
we are the people of the bus
driven to the days of madness
its sadness to see
how the ways of the beast appeals to us
and as the dice is cast
we cast our votes then learn to trust
I say
we've been in this land far far too long now

Most did not plan to come here
but now that we're here
why don't we come together and plan
instead
we sing our sad sad songs
once lamentation
now they profit from our blues
used and abused
we creep the streets confused
auditioning for starring roles
on the six o'clock news
as starving souls abandoned the road of hope
and seek comfort in the demon dope

our sad songs no longer lift us up
our cup remains filled with bitter drink
prayers go unanswered
for we refuse to think
we no longer seek wisdom from above
our brothers and sisters we refuse to love
I say
we've been in this land far far too long now

Too many years of broken promises
have passed the way of the Black man
and as we pass away too soon one by one
who will be left to guide the Black sons?
when the fortitude of the Black woman
that has seen us thru
too many years of enslavement
lays beaten and broken
dying on these western-pavements
she no longer sees the rainbow
she hides her eyes behind tinted windows
no longer sees the light at the end of the tunnel
this vessel by which generations came to be
seeks to end it all
I say we've been in this land far far too long now

We're caught up in the game of do or die
waiting to be caught up in the rapture from the sky
but now as we approach this final chapter
the beasts desperately campaigns
for what he's been after
with confused mind we cast our votes
notes of agony echoing in our past

electing to elect guardians
to a cursed and doomed land
a land of despair
where our fears grow year after year
we forgot that this land
was born of unrighteous labor
on the spilled blood of the brave
and the tortured enslaved
on the tears of our raped queens
shed under the full moon
and the sweat that poured
down our backs in hi-noon
on the broken legs of the Kuntas
who seeked freedom
and castrated hope
that carried seeds of wisdom

This is the land that time did not forget
as in the days of Sodom
her judgement comes
how many righteous souls
will we find in Congress
there has been no progress
no matter who be President
the White House will still be the "White House"
Black Panthers still labeled a dangerous gang
while the klan runs rampant throughout the land

We close our eyes to the truth
ignoring the facts
hiding our eyes behind tinted windows
offering each other no eye contact
I say
we've been in this land far far too long now

The Poet's Word

Caution
this is an explicit poem
where expletives become words
like explosives exploding on the battlefield
                                                  in this poem
                      you will see what the drummer saw
                   and hear what the drummer has to say
                              this is the poets way
                 walking in the vast expanse of ways
                 many days unfold as bridges are built
between this word and that word
stirred into action but not shaken
moving towards the unmovable

                This is what the drummer saw
                   the poet's way is back
                 back to that which came before
to see what the drummer saw
to see the prophets stoned then murdered
because they dared to bring the Spoken Word
to see the innocent faces of the children of Soweto
to see their flames violently extinguished
to see the messiahs nailed to the trees
to free the spirits of those who were killed
but never died
to still the tongue of those who lied
those who spied
and sold us in the night
this is the word
this is the poet's way

This is what the drummer saw
the poet's way is in the future
to teach the children
to reach for knowledge
found within not in college
that true education is a key
that unlocks the door to the inner-me
to know the true enemy
this is the word
this is the poet's way

This is what the drummer saw
the poet's way is now
now is the time
to tell the drug dealers
to let our people go
you are killing your own people
you hypocrites
you crackers whore crack dealing
pimple on a donkey's ass
your ass is busted
you can't be trusted
not around our women
you'll turn them out into street walkers
fast talkers and cash money stalkers
your ass is busted
you can't be trusted

not around our children
you'll have them playing with cops and robbers
for real
they won't even feel
the pain they'll be causing
but you'll be cruising

                                now is the time
                    to tell the brothers to stop
                        stop abusing the sisters
                  treating them worse than shit
          hitting on them when shit gets to stinking
                        thinking he be the shit
                            naught but a sell out
                    he needs to get to hell-out
                          out of all our lives

                      Now is the time
              to tell the children the truth
            that the way is in the word
          that the way is the poet's way
          this is what the drummer saw
         that the poet's way is the word
                              word

Martin Beyond

These words
have gathered themselves together
on these pages
not for to praise Martin
but to honor him
to tell him thank you
for a valiant effort
to remember him
as he appeared unto us
a man who stood for, preached for
marched for non-violence
a man who so loved his people
that he sacrificed his own mortal existence
as a ransom for their freedom
a man with a vision of world peace and harmony
this man Martin was an honorable man
not yet perfect in ways
but seeked after the ways of perfection

These words
have gathered themselves together
on these pages
with a purpose of gratitude and reverence
they too contain an all-consuming passion for Justice
as Martin did
they too seek to awaken in a people
the divine fabric of wisdom
as Martin did

                    they too hunger for
                              the truth
                      the whole truth
           and nothing but the truth
                        as Martin did
     they too search un-tiringly for the path
                    to the promise land
                        as Martin did

But these words seek to do more
they seek to go beyond the grave
to cross over into the land of our dreams
where the scheme of things are seen
as they really are
and by far we see who we really are
hear now the voice of Martin from beyond

        "My people my beloved people I tried
       there was conceived in me divine passion
         a mission to restore a lost people
              to the God of their creation
     but you see where there's good, there is also evil
       and this evil has interwoven a web of deception
                 into the very religion
          that has replaced that old-time religion
            the religion of our ancient ancestors
                 this new-time religion
             was conjured up by the same beast
                  that wanders to and fro
        seeking innocent souls on which to feast

this new-time religion
has cunningly excluded
all references to our ancient way
it fails to speak of creation
from an Afrikan centered point of view
it casts man in the role of an isolated soul
isolated from the sun, the moon, and the stars
this new-time religion is not of life
but of death
forgive me my people
my beloved people
I really tried

But let not my dying be in vain
learn from my mistakes
don't follow me footstep for footstep
for my footsteps will only lead to death
I was remiss in that I could not see

I could not see
that divine Justice could not be found
in the court houses of this land
that divine wisdom did not reside
in the White House of the white man
that divine truth was not written
in the Declarations and Constitutions of this country
that we should in fact
hold certain truths to be evidence of self
that though all men are created equally
all men are not created equal

No more than the river holds the same potential
as the sea
no more than the stars are created equal in power
to the sun
no more than every gale of wind
blows with the same force

So I say unto you my people
that this divine Justice you seek
this divine wisdom you seek
this divine truth you seek
cannot be found without paying a divine price
that this divine price does not require
that you bleed to be freed
but that we pray less with our mouths
and meditate more in our hearts
this divine price means
being in this world but not of this world
this divine price demands
that we Journey deep deep within
towards the consciousness of the God-mind
and therein find the promised land

Now I know that you will go thru
many red seas of doubt
when you make it on thru
divine Justice will be your reward
I know that you will face
many wildernesses of despair and despondency
remember that one cannot live by bread alone
but by every spoken word from the Most High

this is the key to divine wisdom
I know that you will come to
many cross roads of decisions
it is here that fear is crucified
it is here that divine truth is found
and it is this truth that will set you free
I know that one day you will get to the promise land
and when you do my beloved people
remember me Martin'

These words have gathered themselves together
on these pages
to remember Martin
to remember that he tried
he truly tried.

Truth Rises

Marcus Garvey said it, Benjamin Banneker wrote about it, Malcom X believed it, Martin Luther King Jr. died for it. The truth impresses that a man is free despite his physical limitations. All of the great leaders were stressing a point and sending a message by lifting their voices and exercising their basic rights in the face of adversity. It is quite possible to bound a man's hands, it is quite possible to bound his feet, it is even possible to restrict his tongue, but it is totally impossible to bound the soul of man There, I said it, let's face it. While so many of us were killed for the cause of freedom, the Truth is, we have always been free, and will always remain free. While it is impossible for the enemy to bound our souls, it is quite possible for us to be lied to, brainwashed and totally misled.

Yes, we were told a big lie, about us not being free just because we were physically bound. We were brainwashed into believing it, which took close to four hundred years to accomplish. You see, even though we were lied to, it remained a possibility that the truth would surface. To remove this possibility we had to be actively brainwashed, that's right, our brains had to be washed.

Our innate culture was suppressed, any child would testify that a people's culture is a direct result of their perception of the truth.

Aha, so now that we have been actively brainwashed why not just leave us alone you say. Check it out, even in our brainwashed state, we still posed a threat, because truth is the light and there is no way in heaven, on earth, or in hell, that darkness can ever dispel the Light. It just doesn't work that way. So they spent over four hundred years trying to hide us from the truth. They took us from our land, brought us to a foreign climate, and proceeded with their costly game of "hide and come seek".

"As a man thinketh, so is he". Their whole trip was to convince us that we were less than ourselves. Since comparison between ourselves and themselves were impossible based on the fact that you cannot compare the truth to the lie. The physical chains that were placed on our bodies were designed to draw us out of our spiritual nature and focus our attention solely on the physical. The whips against our backs offered us no time to return to a spiritual frame of mind. It gave us no time to catch our breaths. Everything that was done to us was designed to bring us out of our spiritual nature and into their world where they were the masters. This my friends, is known as actively brainwashing, since there is nothing subliminal about it.

In their world, they kill for sport. Check it out, we were misled to dying for spiritual freedom when it was only our physical bodies that were restrained. We were effectively tricked. Consider this, the physical rotates on the numeric (6) while the spiritual world rotates on the number of completion and beginning (0). So you see, to draw us out our spiritual nature, they simply had to brainwash us into being totally concerned about our physical self, which is characterized by a yearning for equality. We had to give up the quest to be God-like.

Black Mother Spirit

And just as the early morning dew
is welcomed by the waiting petals of the spring flower
so too must these words find you
and crown you civilization's mother

    For as surely as the sun retreats daily from the sky
and nightly the moon takes her rightful place on high
you'll always be there

And though I was not present in form
when the crack of that whip
guided by the hands of an over-anxious
obnoxious White terrorist
lashed into the beautiful black skin
of that young Nubian Prince
separating flesh from bone
you were there

    For you helped ease the pain
the pain that tortured his broken body that day
and in the midnight hour
when his spirit threatened to break asunder
you whispered strength from a thousand warriors
in his ear
and his spirit was born again

And with your beautiful dreaded locks you dried
the tears that refused to be shed as he bled
but instead
waited patiently till the deep stillness of the night
yes, you were there

    And though I was not present in form
   when those misguided, distrained hounds
   under the influence of those aboriginal clowns
    ripped apart the very bones of yet another
        Nubian Prince
        you were there

And ignoring the whips that tore at your flesh
you knelt at his side
your tears of love mixed with his agonizing blood
formed a sweet elixir
that nourished the very soil of the cotton fields
you cradled him in your arms
and just as he pursed his lips to curse at God
you whispered in his ear
hold on, be strong and of good courage
and his soul was born again

     And yet again I was not present in form
   when molded lead fled the chambers the AK's
      armed with intent of murder
     from the hearts of the jackal force
  shattered the dreams, the hopes, the very lives
       of our children of Soweto
        you were there

To help bury their small bodies in mother earth
and pray their innocent souls
safely on their ancestral journey
you were there

                        And when I was present in form
         growing to knowing in the backwoods countryside
               on a small island off the coast of Trinidad
                                you were there

For it was you that dressed my skinned knee
and hearkened to my hungry plea
it was you that prayed and stayed the hand of death
when all seemed lost
and in my deepest hour
when manhood abandoned the ways of the child
it was your words of encouragement
and your loving and nurturing ways
your inspiring warm hugs
that founded my memories
and encouraged me to be born again and again

                            And if for no other reason
             than the inbred unwavering love of a mother
         a mother who has given birth to not just a son
        a mother who has given birth to not just a people
              a mother who has given birth civilization

I know that you'll always be there
even when I'm not present in form
and I love you for it
Beautiful Black Mother Spirit.

Turn Right at the Light

You stay right there in your wrong
swear you're right when you're wrong
but two wrongs don't make it right
when you're too right to see you're wrong
when the book you read ain't right
then you too are wrong
when asked if ere thing alright
you say nothing is wrong
so I ask you what's wrong
you say you're all right
that means nothing is left
and that ain't right
that makes you dead wrong
but you can still live right
turn right at the light
what's left is the truth
with that you'll never go wrong
and that's all right

I'm Just Saying

You're the soft-one
the one who has sold-out
the soul-less shell of a creation
turned inside out

You're the wanna-be general
selling that white horse-shit around the way
while poor Black mothers hold funerals
you're in it for the devils pay

                                  Now I'm not even trying to say
                                       that in this day and time
                                          I'm not trying to get mine
                                                 I'm just saying
                    there has to be more to the getting
                            than just making end$
           far more than the Lex coupes and the Benz
                                  there's authentic friends
                                             and family
                                               loved ones
                                          beloved ones
                                           above ones
                                    and beyond ones

The ancients tell of treasures stored up
that no dead presidents can find
they're blind
always have been
even when they were living

There's knowledge, understanding, and wisdom
go inside you and get you some
there's truth, culture, and equality
you've got to know your true self-identity
find within you God's likeness
the power to build is within you
so too is the power to destroy
these are everlasting treasures
more valuable than man-made toys

When you seek after these treasures brother
there'll be no need for shotgun drivebys
no need for fronting, games, and lies
no place in your mind
for those homicidal, suicidal thoughts
your mind will be your heaven
kept cool by a thousand butterflies
flapping their wings
serenaded by a chorus of Soweto children
rising from the dust to sing

Your mind will be transformed
from the hell it is today
and you too will be able to say
to hell with the devil's pay
I'm just saying.

<u>Rise Up</u>

In this poem
you may find words that offend
not like guns but roses
proses of beauty that stems
from the soil of the harsh reality
a reality that fosters a negative identity
an identity torn at the soul
as the thorns of oppression grow sharper
and dark days grow darker

                                                                                        In this poem
words will not pretend
to be less than what they intend
per chance they aspire to inspire
those who desire to go higher
and those who seek not to know
will go the way of stray dogs
with head hung low
and no
dog is not my best friend
turn the word around
this world upside down
and god is at the other end

                                                                                        In this poem
it is not the intent of the writer to preach
nor stand on a pedestal
and deliver a grandiose speech

but to drop knowledge and teach
for each one must reach one
and teach one
for this is not the time
to be concerned about your time
but these times ought to concern us

        For these are the times
        in which of every ten Black men
        the HIV is positive of its victims

                These are the times
                in which our little Black boys
                our little Black girls
                are choosing the style of coffin
                they wish to be buried in

These are the times
in which Black families
are rapidly becoming extinct
and concentration enslavement camps
are on the rise

                These are the times
                the Blackest Panther must roar
                our voices must mount up
                as on the wings of eagles and soar
                soar to the highest mountain top
                and shout into the night
                Stop!!!

                    Stop pissing away your time
                      along with your mind
                    stop sucking that devil's dick
                         it's symbolic
                       it's all a damn trick
                         drop that pipe
                    you shouldn't be holding it

                   Over four hundred years of oppression
                                    has taken its toll
                          you have abandoned all hope
                                 looked to the dope
                          your dreams have grown old
                                        yes its true
                            what I'm saying to you
                     some of us will be lost to the beast
                    we must once again look to the East

In this poem you will read words that demand
that you rise up and take a stand
hear the word
let your thoughts be stirred
set in motion
the revolution of the mind
this is our time Black man
rise up
take a stand
we need you.

The Dinnertime man

I be that dinner-time man
the be there on time man
don't mind changing a diaper
then setting the table for dinner time man
I'll even pull back the cover for bedtime
and get mine
while you get yours

Passions run hot behind closed doors
clothes drop to hard-wood floors
hard-wood delivered as you drop to all fours
fools rush in
but I takes my time
shivers of prolonged quivers pleasurate your spine
cause truth be told
I be that dinner-time man

Slippery tip slid slowly pass tightly held grip
guttural groans uttered thru clenched teeth
quivering lips
measure for measure
rhythmic strokes found your treasure
back arched
your tunnel filled with pleasure

Echoes of waterfalls echoed from behind
Roy Ayers crooned 'everybody loves the sunshine'

We rose together
and sank together
flesh to flesh
we sang together
sweat to sweat
we ate together
you bucked
I gushed
we screamed
then hushed
dinner has been served
by the dinnertime man

Queen

You are the woman in me
standing before me
the outer representation
of my inner beauty
the aspect of my divinity
that I love, honor, and respect
the source of my creativity
you are the power in me
that moves my thoughts to reality
I make this promise to you
I won't try to outshine you
contrary to ill-mental
I'll put you on a pedestal
I'll reverence my ways to you
I come with royal references to you
I refer to scriptures not yet scripted
come let us make man

The Art of Noise

When silence dies
so too does our right to be
our rite to see within
without the noise from without
the shouts of Jubilance
born with the screams of the newborn
whose tender lungs filled with air
feels no fear
expresses itself as the art of noise
fresh from the living silence of the womb
you to whom the Joyful songs proclaim
our ancestor come again

When silence dies
lies live in the crevices of the human soul
bells toll no more from atop high places
where low minds occupy sacred spaces
displacing minds high in thought
like those who fought
for our right to be
our rite to see within
our right to say stop!
kill the noise void of art
let silence live
and ring from every mountain top
as the art of noise

So Far

When will we stop being so late
showing up when shit's over with
we be builders of the shit that's built
but not sellers of it
merely consumers of it
always late even to your own funerals
saluting parasites as generals
too late to save the Kings
the Malcoms and the Garveys
can we save our destinies?
roasted in fires on plantations
plantations fired us
we went right back to it
put our backs to it
built them roads and inroads
rail roads, rodeos, free-throws
we built them death rows
we gave them themes for plays
built them ways
to do things
yet we have no-things
but it's not too late today
some say yesterday
like Sankofa
but so far we ain't been but so far

New Pages are Born

I've written them in the trees
that man will not live by bread alone
but by degrees
the mental keys
unlocking doors to distant shores
Moors come with codes
to those who are not yet born
deceivers deciphering without the book
they see not where to look
these words got them shook
I stand in the company of Gods
casting long and brilliant shadows
my pupils come dilated
from seeing my peoples die lately
choke-holds to forty-one shots
they're killing us loudly
then they take to mics and apologize softly
I've written them in the trees
this is the dawn of new ages
while young pages are too soon bourne
new pages continue to be born
I've written them in the trees

Our Support Supports

It is our support that supports
the very foundation of our destruction
we've been shrink wrapped
like drums of black oil on white shelves
we are tapped
souls drained dry
come now trapped
some strapped from head to toe
they draw the map
we follow
the map that leads to sesame street
they say it's easy street
where our futures are easy meat
a treat for the beasts in suits
we've been tricked into minding our own business
but we have few businesses to mind
keep in mind
it's our support that supports
the very foundation of our destruction

Hypocrites

Many regurgitate preconceived thoughts
generate tongue twisting talk
the talk the label tells them to talk
they fail to walk beyond the talk
walking the walk of the hypocrite
their words are but pleasantly sounding rhetoric
mentally invasive bullshit
reptilian brains attracted to the way they said it
like the gun slinger fast on the draw
can't shoot straight
much fancy footwork
they'll call this hate
cause the truth hurts

They hopped on rocks to pay for their demo
now they're riding in rooftop limos
say they did it for the babies
but children don't need no Jordans
they need their mother back
can you do that?
she's the one tapping on your wind shield
offering to suck you off for twenty
you turned her out when she was twenty
now you got plenty
and the children are left empty
so they consume your bass-backed bullshit
can't digest it so they regurgitate it
all they got to show for it
is how to be a hypocrite

Surprised Again

As if teleported to a different time and place
far, far away yet seemingly nearby
my body sleeps, my mind awake, occupying space
within my dream, or was I?

The setting seemed pleasant
tall trees green grass
Afrikan families gathered together with Europeans
eating, drinking, laughing, playing
completely relaxed
we felt no need for defense
we told ourselves they were our friends

Slowly but suddenly all the Whites fled
just White flight we said
we hardly realized we were isolated
corralled like cattle we were relegated
like educated fools we come now dis-educated
once again in the hands of others we placed our trust
we have been tricked into ignoring past tortures
integrating, assimilating
striving to please everyone but us
without a warning
the beast in it's true form appeared
like hell from the clouds
he rained down huge boulders
there was a sudden change in our community

a sense of fear
black men and women crushed to death
with the weight of a brutal and hostile world
on their shoulders

Mothers searching for their children
while the piper pied
grown men running, screaming no place to hide
what remains of our culture
on the verge of destruction
we trusted the European before
it led to our abduction
weak off-springs produced as families divide
homes torn apart where no father resides

Only a few survive the one sided fight
a place to regroup is our destiny
we make our way under the cover of night
creeping the back roads avoiding pawns of the enemy
the end is near
we must find peace within each other or die
this I saw while in a dream
or was I?

3/8/93

The Cast-Aways

From the day they were born
some children are merely spawned
craving mother's breasts
life lines below distress
dropped from the womb like a heavy burden
tell me, who weeps for these children?

>It matters not who's to blame
it matters that they are here
some maybe the result of violence
yet others a frivolous affair
some are used for income then forgotten
tell me who weeps for these children?

We are destroying today our tomorrows
blaming them for all our sorrows
some found in garbage cans others in ovens
tell me, who weeps for these children?

>On the wings of vultures
the evil from the crack world flies strong
selective in its flight it seeks the young
unsuspecting and trusting they embrace the end
tell me, who weeps for these children?

Will we ever stop slaughtering the innocent
will we ever weep for ourselves?

The Sea Saw Me

The rain fell
she would swell
inviting me with her smell
I would lay on her banks
giving thanks
as I drank

To my feet she sent her wave
calling me into her cave
I had to be brave
I graced her tide
with a leap and a stride
into her waiting depth to hide

The Struggle Continues

As brother is trained to guard brother the struggle intensifies. Families torn further apart, children needlessly and senselessly slaughtered in the streets, and brother guarding brother. The pain runs deep. All seems hopeless, for our oppressors possess means by which total annihilation of our people seems possible. They are the minority, but the weapons and political backing they have makes the difference critical. Yet the struggle continues. Lives are given for the cause, in the name of peace. Our oppressors rejoice with every drop of blood that's shed. They laugh at the fact that we do not employ great military means that will enable us to force a compromise. Yet, the struggle continues.

We are reminded of the days of the cowboys and Indians. The Indians would attack with spears and arrows, while the cowboys laid in wait. Entrenched with canoes and automatic means of destruction. They envy us for the simple ideals we stand for. For the way we care for each other. For the way we raise and educate our young. For the way we care for our elders. They came amongst us with this deep envy an envy so deep it looks and feels like hate, and because of our supreme nature we gave to them without charging. They brought their laws and their guns, and while we slept, they crept in and took up post.

We awoke years later and found ourselves the object of terrorism within our own land. we were told that this was for the good of all. That we were inept at handling our own affairs, running our own lives, managing our own land, which we have been doing since the inception of man millions of years ago.

Their plan is to erase our culture from the face of the earth, for without culture, a people can never be certain of the truth, and without that certainty, that people may unwittingly trade their souls into bondage. This is why the European was planted in places like South Africa and the Congo, and given powerful support by the super-violent nations to ensure their success in terrorizing the African and erasing his culture from the roots, from his very homeland. Never mind America, or England, for if the homeland is lost, we have no point of reference beyond the shores of America. And who is responsible for ledgering American history? not us. This is why we as American born Africans, and European born Africans, and Caribbean born Africans must make every conscious effort to keep the struggle alive. As a fish when taken out of water struggles with every ounce of life left in its body to return to its environment of Life, so too we must fight to regain the knowledge of our culture, of who we are in relation to any other man on earth. The struggle must continue.

Awareness

It is a light that shines brightly in the mind. Dispelling the darkness of ignorance from every crevice, and every corner. Instilling an aura of good feeling about one's self in the face of disparity and envy from without. To know the inner self is to be aware, aware of the potential to build or to destroy, whichever becomes necessary for the enhancement of Life.

The Light that is awareness can readily be observed from without. It is evident in one's attitude and behavior. There are those who are also of the light, who will do everything in their power to enhance the growth of another. Beware of the negative mind draped in a layer of positivity. They are destructive and malicious by nature. Their ultimate purpose is to dim the Light that shines brightly in the mind.

The sense of awareness brings with it a lonely atmosphere. It is must easier to be unaware, for practically no effort is required to be unaware, most importantly, far less responsibility is assumed by those who are unaware. Because those who are unaware by far outnumber those who are aware. There is a strong incentive to be counted amongst the unaware. One can always find another like mind to relate to amongst the unaware.

Natural Man Awake

Long is the night of despair and sorrow
each moment seems an eternity til the morrow
yet, somehow, hope finds fertile soil within the soul
growing, showing the way, to the whole

            Strong we must be, for we are to be
      protectors of our people, their visionary
                seeing before it has come
        the resurrection of our African kingdom.

Patient we must be, for we are to lead
the minds of our people
away from the grasp of greed
humbling ourselves to the least of us
developing in our God the binding trust

            Wise we must be, for we must judge
    the actions of our brother let none be-grudge
        accepting the burden for our future's sake
      this is our destiny, oh natural man awake.

Brother's Keepers

My brothers don't need no keeping
too many kept behind bars as it is
too many kept from being born
to the tree of life they just piss on
their world is a world of dogs
they be the baddest on the block
matter of fact
they be the only dogs on their blocks
all other men be their masters
from the corner-stores to the liquor-stores
they fail to see the disasters

My brothers don't need no keeping
they need to strip that over-priced bling
put on sackcloth and ashes
then get to weeping
weep for the many sisters they sold into slavery
slavery to a myriad of control substances
to a life dependent on table dances
my brothers need to get to weeping
weeping for the seeds they flung haphazardly
into the deep dark soil of the womb
seeds nourished with blood
but not nurtured with a father's love
seeds that are seeds no more but life
formed in the manifestation
of the Creator's intention
a man-child perhaps
left to face a cruel and unjust world
without the hand of his father to guide him
my brothers ought to be weeping
weep for themselves

wash their feet in the tears of remembrance
submerge their self-pity
their commercialized self-degradation
their conditioned self-hate
submerge themselves in the knowledge of self
my brothers don't need no keeping
my brothers be keeping my brothers
from weeping.

Sow Your Seeds Well

We once focused on being sages
now just characters on stages
actors of rages
minds trapped on pages
rehearsals of Hamlet regurgitated
then serve over easy
hold the intensity
just entertain me
with metaphors lacking power
like flash showers
hold the thunderstorm
thoughts consumed
before they are born
we have a long way to go
and a short time to get there
so excuse me if I don't care to be well-known
I prefer that these words are well-sown

THE NEXT TEST OF MEN

Coming next
Coming next
Coming next
Coming next
Coming next
Coming next
Coming next
Coming next
Coming next
Coming next
Coming next
Coming next
Coming next
Coming next

Dam That Habit

www.ingramcontent.com/pod-product-compliance
Lightning Source LLC
Chambersburg PA
CBHW070318230426
43663CB00011B/2174